Fashion Illustration

Edited by Chai Xiuming and Lu Haoyang

DESIGN MEDIA PUBLISHING LIMITED

©2010 by Design Media Publishing Limited
This edition published in May 2011

Design Media Publishing Limited
20/F Manulife Tower
169 Electric Rd, North Point
Hong Kong
Tel: 00852-28672587
Fax: 00852-25050411
E-mail: Kevinchoy@designmediahk.com
www.designmediahk.com

Editing: Xiuming Chai & Haoyang Lu
Proofreading: Katy Lee
Cover Design: Coraline Cao
Design/Layout: Cong Zhao & Coraline Cao

ISBN 978-988-19739-5-5

Printed in China

Contens

Pencil & Line

Pencil lines are drawn with pencil, including drawings and sketches and so on. Line is the most important technique of expression among the pencil drawings, which develops rapidly with various styles and types. Pencil lines used in the clothing illustration are also distinctive: virtual or real, thick or thin, deep or shallow, strong or light ...

According to the pursuit of different illustrators, the lines could be energetic or delicate, awkward or smooth, light or dark ... various options to achieve the best expression. Illustrators employ the coherent, lively, varied and rhythmic lines to give a sense of fashion, expressing the beauty of discreet luxury.

⊕ Alexandra Kaegler
UK

Title: Elegance of Simplicity
Media: pencil on paper, Photoshop editing

Elegance is fluid and therefore by definition difficult to define, but it is made of desire and
knowledge, of grace, refinement, distinction and perfect purity of line.
This spring/summer '10 collection is inspired by the belle epoque period and ballets russes;
well known for its dresses with round collars, little cuffs and full rounded skirts.

⊕ **Adddress**
Germany

⊕ Adddress
Germany

Title: In Motion
Media: For each project a different technique is used to emphasise the theme
as well as possible.

The Fall Winter 2009.2010 collection is called "In Motion" and outlines the
process of dressing in general, which is linked to the label name "adddress".
The inspiration for the collections in general comes from the surroundings of
the idea of the label itself.

⊕ **Adddress**
Germany

⊕ Adddress
Germany

Title: In Motion
Media: For each project a different technique is used to emphasise the theme
as well as possible.

The Fall Winter 2009.2010 collection is called "In Motion" and outlines the
process of dressing in general, which is linked to the label name "adddress".
The inspiration for the collections in general comes from the surroundings of
the idea of the label itself.

⊕ **Adddress**
Germany

Title: In Motion
Media: For each project a different technique is used to emphasise the theme as well as possible.

The Fall Winter 2009.2010 collection is called "In Motion" and outlines the process of dressing in general, which is linked to the label name "adddress". The inspiration for the collections in general comes from the surroundings of the idea of the label itself.

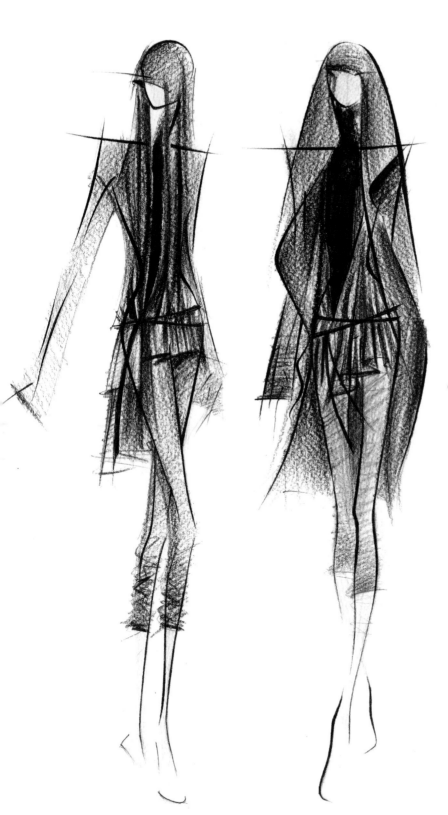

⊕ **Anca Georgiana Lungu**
Romania

Title: The Midnight Call
Media: coloured pencils and black ink, except the
        man which was drew in Illustrator.

The black silhouettes are two sketches the
designer did for the graduation master collection,
at Polimoda, Italy. The collection was called "The
midnight call" and the designer mostly used soft
leathers and silk, all black. The outfits were inspired
by warrior women fighting evil and were meant for
an avant-garde personality.

DIVYA RAMAN
COLLECTION : VICTORIAN DUPE AW06/07

⊕ **Divya Raman**
UK

Title: Architectural
Media: graphite pencil, Photoshop Lasso tool, Corel Draw, graphic
pen, Felt tips Collections and season are mentioned along side each
illustration.

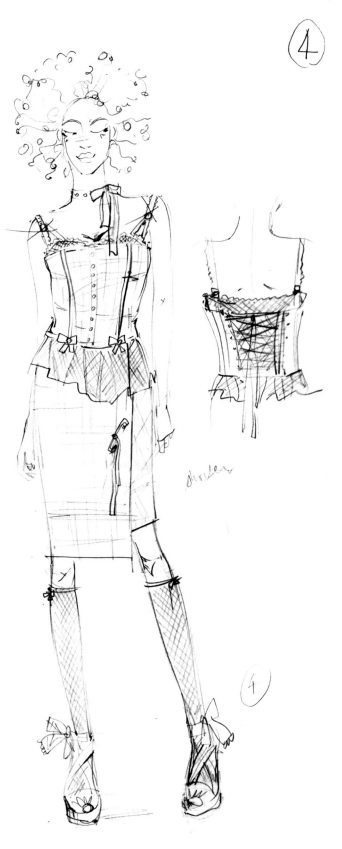

⊕ Elmaz Hüseyin
USA

Title: "Gentlemen's Club" First Sketches
Medium (Sketches): 1B Lead Pencil
Medium (Mood Board): Photoshop

The client was Ecko Red for the FEMME ARSENAL label. The designer was asked to design a capsule collection based on upscale lingerie and gentlemen's clubs. The designer researched and put together a mood board. These are a few of the initial sketches the designer submitted.

A & B

Both
as short
& shirt -

⊕ **Elmaz Hüseyin**
USA

Title: "Gentlemen's Club" First Sketches
Medium (Sketches): 1B Lead Pencil
Medium (Mood Board): Photoshop

The client was Ecko Red for the FEMME ARSENAL label. The designer was asked to design a capsule collection based on upscale lingerie and gentlemen's clubs. The designer researched and put together a mood board. These are a few of the initial sketches the designer submitted.

⊕ Elmaz Hüseyin

USA

Title: "Gentlemen's Club" First Sketches
Medium (Sketches): 1B Lead Pencil
Medium (Mood Board): Photoshop

The client was Ecko Red for the FEMME
ARSENAL label. The designer was asked to
design a capsule collection based on upscale
lingerie and gentlemen's clubs. The designer
researched and put together a mood board.
These are a few of the initial sketches the
designer submitted.

⊕ **Fabiana Pigna**
Los Angeles, CA

Title: Asymmetric
Media: ink and pencil on paper

Part of a collection of drawings, each expressing a state of longing
for a lost love; asymmetry and texture work together to evoke such
feelings.

⊕ **Fabiana pigna**

Los Angeles, CA

Title: Unmasked
Media: ink and pencil on paper

Blinded by a feathered mask, braids and geometric lines become
part of this composition to express the complexity of lost love.

⊕ Fabiana Pigna
Los Angeles, CA

Title: Don't Look Back
Media: ink and pencil on paper

A wide-eyed beauty looks back at the past with
melancholy as leaves and geometric lines form
sublime prints.

⊕ Fabiana Pigna
Los Angeles, CA

Title: Torera
Media: ink and pencil on paper

As she wears the intricate Bullfighter jacket, she's
saddened by the weight of death it carries.

⊕ Muhammad Fawad Noori

Pakistan

Title: B&W
Media: pencil and marker

Once a day the designer was sitting in his office and marking the assignments of pattern made by his students. Feeling very tired, he stopped checking, took an A4 sheet and a lead pencil, and then started making this quick illustration. It's a casual day wear outfit. Then he took marker to outline the illustration to add depth on it.

⊕ Lucy Brickwood
UK

Title: Madness Final Line up
Media: pencil and promarker line drawing on paper

This project is from the collection "could it be madness – this??"
2008 by Lucy Brickwood,UK. The illustration is pencil line drawing on
paper.

⊕ Lucy Brickwood
UK

Title: Mattimo Line up Roughts 4
Media: pencil and promarker line drawing on paper

Illustration from "eccentric cavalier" collection of Mattimo Dutti, 2008, Spain.
This illustration is promarker on paper.
The collection is based on the classic well dressed chic menswear, the swarve
style of Roger Moore's 007 sleek British style and Savile row tailoring and
fabrications with a Charlie Chaplin fit and silhouette.

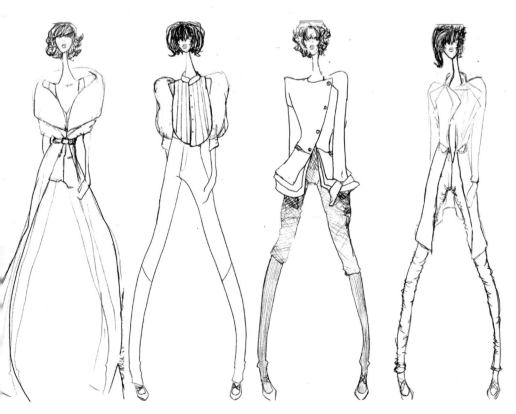

⊕ **Nadja Hermann**

The series numbered with 1, 2, and 3 were inspired by the natural contrast between the life in a small village in the country and a vibrant environment of a big city. They were drawn after visiting an exhibition of works by Henri de Toulouse-Lautrec in Münster, Germany.

⊕ **Nadja Hermann**

drop
the armhole
a little

⊕ Nadja Hermann

The sketches for "men" were inspired by a trip to Stockholm, by the city itself and of course by the incredible men's fashion the designer had to admire being there.

parka

leather/
fabric

jersey

Linen

jeans

Neda Niquie
USA

Title: Call Me Spike
Media: pencil on vellum paper

This image is created specially for a publication.

⊕ **Neda Niquie**
USA

Title: Niya
Media: pencil on paper

This sketch is created specially for a publication, a design from
Spring/Summer Niquie collection

⊕ **Neda Niquie**
USA

Title: Space Pirate
Media: pencil

⊕ Neda Niquie
USA

Title: Untitled
Media: pencil and pen on paper

Some costume sketches for a movie.

Dip Pen

Costume illustrators could apply the delicate single colour lines into the creation so as to highlight the contrast between the black and white tone in the clothing illustrations.

The most beautiful lines of ink strokes are a real expression of mind. The bold and smooth lines with black and white tone could enhance the compactibility of the illustrations and thus achieve fine characterisation of the costumes and characters.

⊕ **Adddress**
Germany

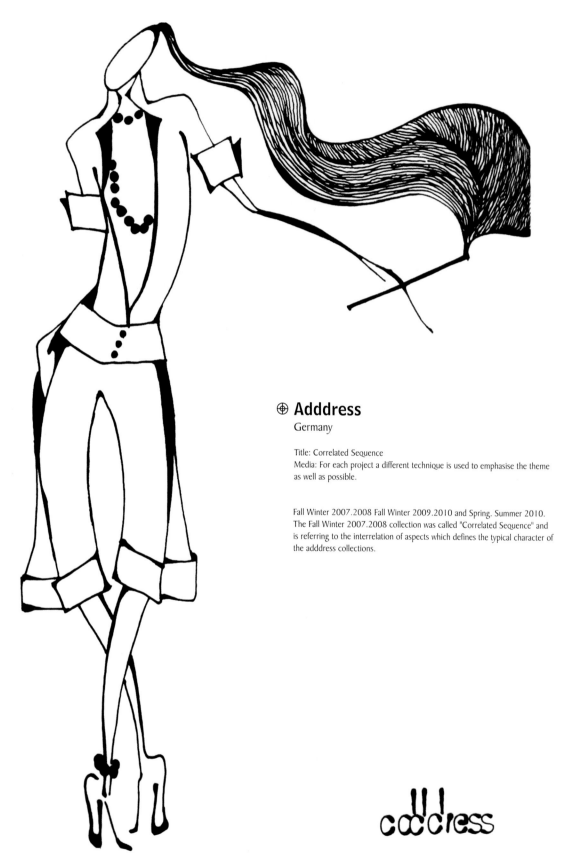

⊕ Adddress

Germany

Title: Correlated Sequence
Media: For each project a different technique is used to emphasise the theme
as well as possible.

Fall Winter 2007.2008 Fall Winter 2009.2010 and Spring. Summer 2010.
The Fall Winter 2007.2008 collection was called "Correlated Sequence" and
is referring to the interrelation of aspects which defines the typical character of
the adddress collections.

⊕ Adddress

Germany

Title: Correlated Sequence
Media: For each project a different technique is used to emphasise the theme
as well as possible.

Fall Winter 2007.2008 Fall Winter 2009.2010 and Spring. Summer 2010.
The Fall Winter 2007.2008 collection was called "Correlated Sequence" and
is referring to the interrelation of aspects which defines the typical character of
the adddress collections.

fake leather

leatherette

FUN FUR . . . .

(fake)
snakeskin
slax . —

stax
SLAX

stripe
down
outside
leg
(ake
snakeskin

CADILLAC
CHAUFFERETTE

Gruvy

©ELMAZ HÜSEYIN

=Keep on truckin =

⊕ **Elmaz Hüseyin**
USA

⊕ **Elena Kikina**
Germany

Title: Firkant
Media: pencil, Adobe Photoshop

⊕ **Elena Kikina**
Germany

⊕ **Elena Kikina**
Germany

Title: Firkant
Media: pencil, Adobe Photoshop

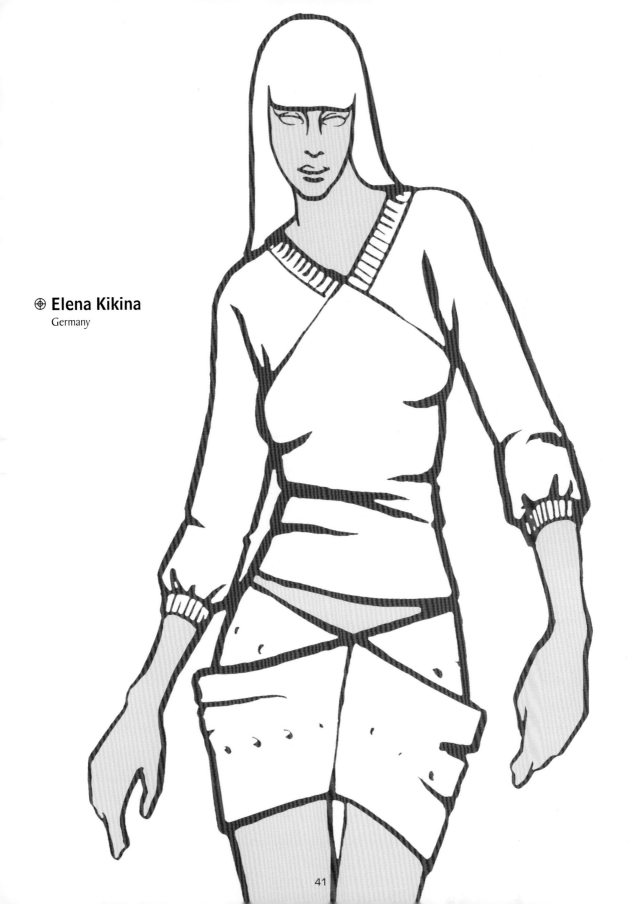

⊕ **Elena Kikina**
Germany

41

⊕ Elmaz Hüseyin
USA

Title: "70'S PIMP" Collection
Media (Black & White Sketches): Indian ink &
drawing pen (Dip Pen) on vellum (Sketches were first
drawn in pencil on layout paper then re-drawn on
vellum using Indian ink and a Dip Pen)
Media (Sketches With Colour): photocopies of pen
& ink drawings onto acetate cell paper and coloured
from the reverse with cell paint and poster pens)

On a trip to NYC in the mid-80's, the designer missed
the stop on the subway and ended up in the South
Bronx. A pimp and one of his girls got on the train.
In the designer's youthful British eyes, the pimp's
clothes seemed like they came right out of an episode
of Starsky & Hutch. ....purple coat, matching hat, big
reveres, snakeskin shoes; she was wearing a big fur
with an amazing do. So this "accidental trip" was the
inspiration for 70's Pimp – one of the designer's earliest
collections.
The designer was so inspired that she started drawing
almost immediately, creating some interesting
characters and situations. However, in her world, it
was the women who were the "pimps" and charge of
themselves – the men were their "accessories".

⊕ Elmaz Hüseyin
USA

Title: Tommy Hilfiger Illustrations
Media: brush pen (Initial drawings were in pencil HB/1B, then re-drawn using a black brush pen).

Some fashion houses use illustrators to work with their design teams who, for the most part nowadays have different skill-sets that require them to be efficient in areas other than illustration. The designer worked with design teams at Tommy Hilfiger helping them to realise their vision for presentations and line adoptions in the absence of prototypes that were perhaps still being made in Asia. The designer used their seasonal colours, got into the feel of the consumer, and added some styling and design touches of her own with shoes, tights, sunglasses, hats, bags & hair.

⊕ Elmaz Hüseyin
USA

Title: Tommy Hilfiger Illustrations
Media: brush pen (Initial drawings were in pencil HB/1B, then re-drawn using a black brush pen).

Some fashion houses use illustrators to work with their design teams who, for the most part nowadays have different skill-sets that require them to be efficient in areas other than illustration.

The designer worked with design teams at Tommy Hilfiger helping them to realise their vision for presentations and line adoptions in the absence of prototypes that were perhaps still being made in Asia. The designer used their seasonal colours, got into the feel of the consumer, and added some styling and design touches of her own with shoes, tights, sunglasses, hats, bags & hair.

⊕ **Elmaz Hüseyin**
USA

⊕ **Ewelina Klimczak**
Poland

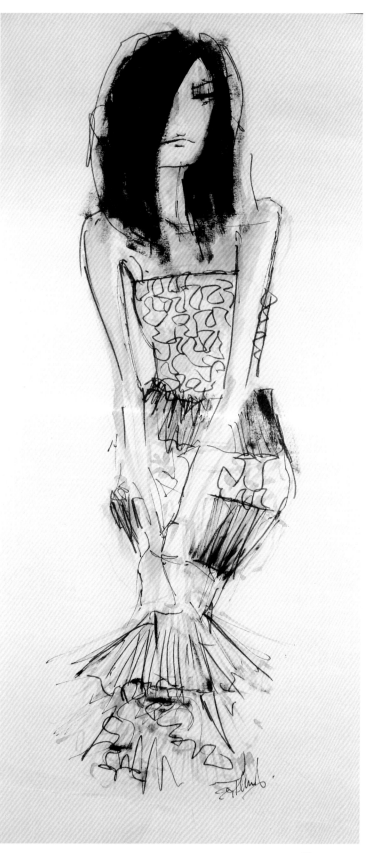

⊕ **Ewelina Klimczak**
Poland

⊕ **Ewelina Klimczak**
Poland

Coloured Pencil

The colour pencil includes non-water-soluble colour pencil and water-soluble colour pencil which is often used in the creation of the fashion illustration. Illustrators often employ them to highlight the space, perspective and shading. In the process of drawing, too much use of the colour pencil could result in the stiffness and dullness of the design. Many clothing illustrators often combine the colour pencil with other tools, such as the pencil lines, by using pencil lines to sketch out the contours of characters, and then colour it with the colour pencil; or with marker pen, which is firstly used to set the tone of the whole design and then combines with the colour pencil to describe the characters deeply; or even with the water colour to vary colour naturally.

⊕ **Alexandra Kaegler**
UK

Title: Architectural
Media: pencil, coloured pencils, fine liner – on paper

The material choices were of the essence, to create structure, stiffness and strong silhouettes. High quality natural fabrics like cotton poplin, wool crepe, leather and fused materials such as the wool/cashmere teflon bonded suiting.

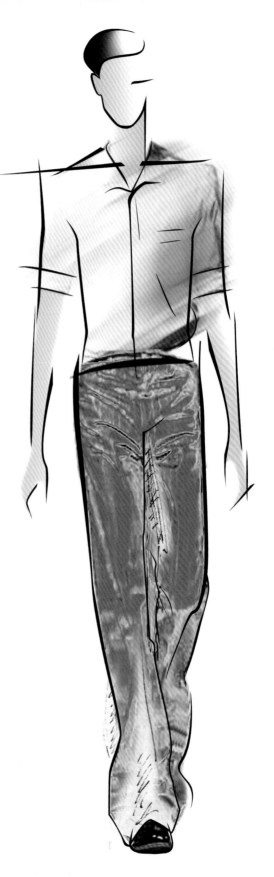

⊕ **Anca Georgiana Lungu**
Romania

Title: Architectural
Media: coloured pencils and black ink, except the
man which was drew in Illustrator.

The other sketches are some proposals of romantic
inspiration with pieces loaded with details, for the
fall-winter 09 collection the designer did for a
fashion house in Constanta, Romania; waist-lenght
jackets, dresses, pants, geometrical shapes in
neutral colours and feminine cuts.

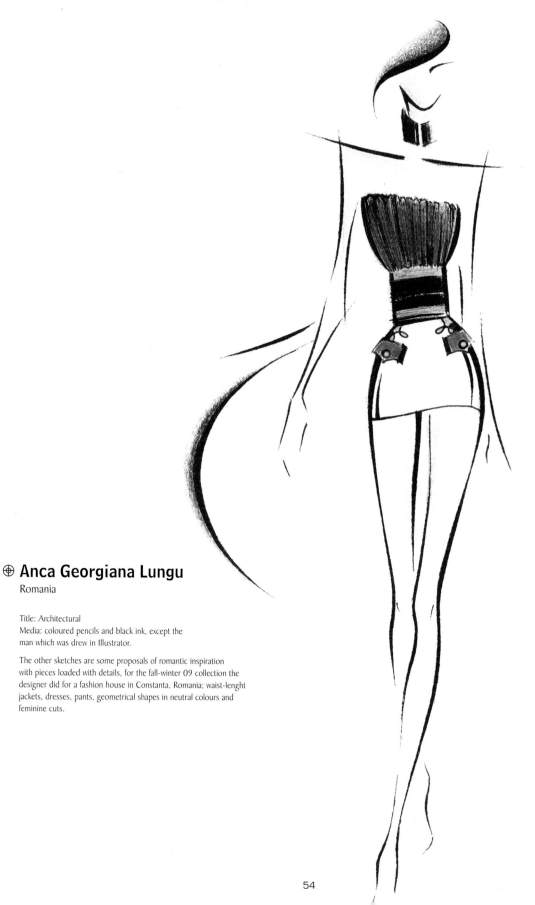

⊕ Anca Georgiana Lungu
Romania

Title: Architectural
Media: coloured pencils and black ink, except the
man which was drew in Illustrator.

The other sketches are some proposals of romantic inspiration
with pieces loaded with details, for the fall-winter 09 collection the
designer did for a fashion house in Constanta, Romania; waist-lenght
jackets, dresses, pants, geometrical shapes in neutral colours and
feminine cuts.

⊕ **Anca Georgiana Lungu**
Romania

⊕ Anca Georgiana Lungu

Romania

Title: Architectural
Media: coloured pencils and black ink, except the
man which was drew in Illustrator.

The other sketches are some proposals of romantic
inspiration with pieces loaded with details, for the
fall-winter 09 collection the designer did for a
fashion house in Constanta, Romania; waist-lenght
jackets, dresses, pants, geometrical shapes in
neutral colours and feminine cuts.

⊕ Elmaz Hüseyin
USA

Title: Tommy Hilfiger Illustrations
Media: Initial roughs were in pencil hb then a heavy black pencil – with cleaner lines – then the designer would photocopy them and add colour using pantone pens, gouache, coloured pencils and sometimes pastels. On the girl's colour sketches, the designer has used watercolour (photocopied then watercolour).

Some fashion houses use illustrators to work with their design teams who, for the most part nowadays have different skill-sets that require them to be efficient in areas other than illustration.
The designer worked with design teams at Tommy Hilfiger helping them to realise their vision for presentations and line adoptions in the absence of prototypes that were perhaps still being made in Asia. The designer used their seasonal colours, got into the feel of the consumer, and added some styling and design touches of her own with shoes, tights, sunglasses, hats, bags & hair.

⊕ **Elmaz Hüseyin**
USA

⊕ Elmaz Hüseyin
USA

Title: Tommy Hilfiger Illustrations
Media: Initial roughs were in pencil hb then a heavy black pencil – with cleaner lines – then the designer would photocopy them and add colour using pantone pens, gouache, coloured pencils and sometimes pastels. On the girl's colour sketches, the designer has used watercolour (photocopied then watercolour).

Some fashion houses use illustrators to work with their design teams who, for the most part nowadays have different skill-sets that require them to be efficient in areas other than illustration.
The designer worked with design teams at Tommy Hilfiger helping them to realise their vision for presentations and line adoptions in the absence of prototypes that were perhaps still being made in Asia. The designer used their seasonal colours, got into the feel of the consumer, and added some styling and design touches of her own with shoes, tights, sunglasses, hats, bags & hair.

⊕ **Elmaz Hüseyin**
USA

Title: Tommy Hilfiger Illustrations
Media: Initial roughs were in pencil hb then a heavy black pencil – with cleaner lines – then the designer would photocopy them and add colour using pantone pens, gouache, coloured pencils and sometimes pastels. On the girl's colour sketches, the designer has used watercolour (photocopied then watercolour).

Some fashion houses use illustrators to work with their design teams who, for the most part nowadays have different skill-sets that require them to be efficient in areas other than illustration.
The designer worked with design teams at Tommy Hilfiger helping them to realise their vision for presentations and line adoptions in the absence of prototypes that were perhaps still being made in Asia. The designer used their seasonal colours, got into the feel of the consumer, and added some styling and design touches of her own with shoes, tights, sunglasses, hats, bags & hair.

⊕ **Elmaz Hüseyin**
USA

⊕ Elmaz Hüseyin
USA

Title: Tommy Hilfiger Illustrations
Media: Initial roughs were in pencil hb then a heavy black pencil – with
cleaner lines – then the designer would photocopy them and add colour
using pantone pens, gouache, coloured pencils and sometimes pastels. On
the girl's colour sketches, the designer has used watercolour (photocopied
then watercolour).

Some fashion houses use illustrators to work with their design teams who,
for the most part nowadays have different skill-sets that require them to be
efficient in areas other than illustration.
The designer worked with design teams at Tommy Hilfiger helping them to
realise their vision for presentations and line adoptions in the absence of
prototypes that were perhaps still being made in Asia. The designer used
their seasonal colours, got into the feel of the consumer, and added some
styling and design touches of her own with shoes, tights, sunglasses, hats,
bags & hair.

⊕ **Elmaz Hüseyin**
USA

⊕ Elmaz Hüseyin
USA

Title: Dama Girl (Kellwood – Phat Fashions)
Media: black & white photocopy & rembrandt pastels

DAMAROUGHELMAZ, DAMACOLOURELMAZ – these sketches were
created as part of launch art for DAMA women's line.
The designers were using flowers as part of the showroom display that they
had bought in Chinatown, which inspired the designer to create a sort of afro
with flowers for the illustration. The designer was also inspired by Naomi
Campbell's features. The designer first drew her on size A3 paper and then
enlarged her to life size on a roller printer.

⊕ Fabiana Pigna

Los Angeles, CA

Title: Tafetán
Media: coloured pencils on paper

Inspired by the texture of silk taffeta and its structural nature.

⊕ Fabiana Pigna

Los Angeles, CA

Title: Jojoto
Media: colour pencils on paper

A tongue-in-cheek drawing about the shoulder pad trend. This girl is so tiny that she's using little corn pieces as her shoulder enhancers.

⊕ Fabiana Pigna
Los Angeles, CA

Title: Chinatown
Media: pencils and Photoshop

A digital drawing inspired by the diversity and modern simplicity of Los Angeles' Chinatown.

⊕ **Fabiana Pigna**
Los Angeles, CA

Title: Louis Vuitton Bust
Media: colour pencils on paper

A drawing inspired by the bunny ears created by Marc Jacobs for the fashion house Louis Vuitton.

⊕ Fabiana Pigna
Los Angeles, CA

Title: Marianita
Media: colour pencils on paper

Close up of a friend wearing an intricate, pleated high shoulder top.

⊕ **Fabiana Pigna**
Los Angeles, CA

Title: The unknown
Media: colour pencils on paper

Inspired by geometric and colour blocking. The figure looks ahead into the unknown.

⊕ Nadja Hermann

The inspiration for the "knit" series has been the contrast of things, compact and loose, stable and fragile form and surface. It is also about searching for a form and shape, not about finding it.

⊕ Nadja Hermann

The inspiration for the "knit" series has been the contrast of things, compact and loose, stable and fragile form and surface. It is also about searching for a form and shape, not about finding it.

⊕ **Nadja Hermann**

The inspiration for the "knit" series has been the contrast of things, compact and loose, stable and fragile form and surface. It is also about searching for a form and shape, not about finding it.

⊕ **Neda Niquie**
USA

⊕ Neda Niquie
USA

Title: A Fantasy at Casa Batllo
Media: coloured pencil, marker pen, water colour
on paper

Sketches from a collection inspired by Antonio
Gaudi's Casa Batllo.

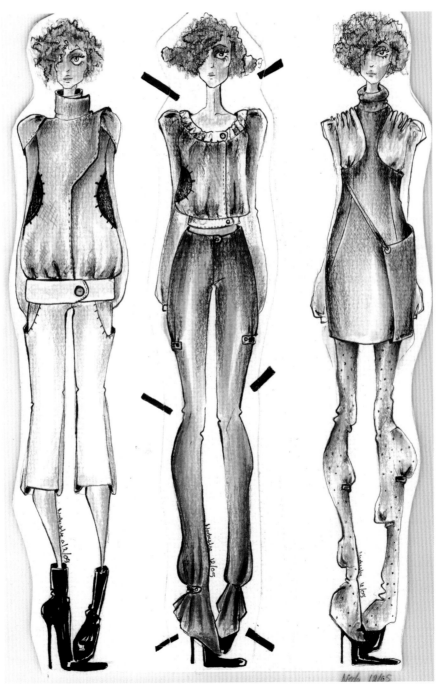

⊕ **Neda Niquie**
USA

⊕ Neda Niquie
USA

Media: pencil, coloured pencils and pen on paper

This sketch created specially for a publication, a design from Spring/
Summer 2009 Niquie collection

⊕ Neda Niquie
USA

Title: Elvish Fashionistas
Media: water colour, coloured pencils and marker
pens on paper

This piece orignally was made for an art exhibition in
Istanbul in 2008. The designer usually creates some
fictional characters and tells a story around them; she
is also fascinated by fairy characters, so she pictured
three elves in some futuristic look.

⊕ Neda Niquie

USA

Title: Mothers of War
Media: water colour, coloured pencils and marker
pens on paper

These two sketches are from a collection in 2006.

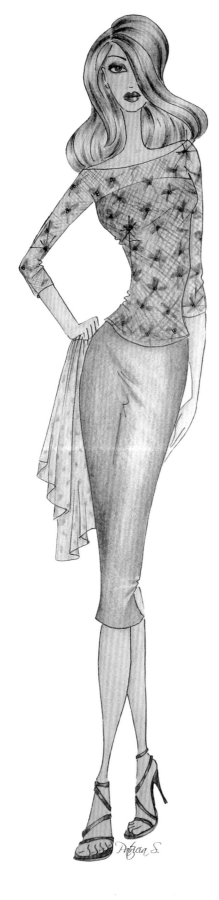

⊕ **PB design**

⊕ **PB design**

Patrizia S.

⊕ **PB design**

Patricia S.

⊕ **PB design**

⊕ **PB design**

Patrizia S.

⊕ Shivani Gakhar
India

Title: A Little Further away from Lightning (A collection inspired by Lightning)
Media: pen, oil pastel crayons, Photoshop

White raw silk shirt, violet shot silk skirt, woolen long trench coat and blue tights
with black and silver leather boots.
Technique used: Paper cuts with fabric under it.

⊕ Shivani Gakhar

India

Title: Experiments with Crayons and Backgrounds
Media: pen, oil pastel crayons, Photoshop

The Threepenny Opera
Mrs. Peachum

Yan Fong

⊕ **YAN FONG**

⊕ YAN FONG

Title: Penny 7,4,3,2,8
Name: Three Penny Opera Custom Design
Media: colour pencil, Photoshop

This is a collection for a theatre play named "The Three Penny Opera" which is about an antiheroic criminal. The aim of the illustration is to present the deepest desire of each actor and it challenges traditional environment and modern style. Therefore the designer uses the tone of dark romance as the signature colour with the lace embellishment in order to create the mood of 30s. The background also adds the darkness to the corner of the street which might create a mystery atmosphere for audience.

Yan Fong

The Threepenny Opera
whore

The Threepenny Opera
Polly Peachum

The Threepenny O
Jenny Diver

⊕ YAN FONG

Title: Penny 7,4,3,2,8
Name: Three Penny Opera Custom Design
Media: colour pencil, Photoshop

This is a collection for a theatre play named "The Three Penny Opera" which is about an antiheroic criminal. The aim of the illustration is to present the deepest desire of each actor and it challenges traditional environment and modern style. Therefore the designer uses the tone of dark romance as the signature colour with the lace embellishment in order to create the mood of 30s. The background also adds the darkness to the corner of the street which might create a mystery atmosphere for audience.

⊕ YAN FONG

⊕ YAN FONG

Title: 6.8 in 1
Name: The 60s girls
Media: colour pencil, Photoshop, Illustrator

Inspired by 60s Mary Quant's fashion style. Using all
the welcoming colours like bright yellow, lime green,
white, charming orange to create a happy and joyful
mood. The position is also a link to make the party
alive; it links up every individual position as a whole
picture.

⊕ YAN FONG

Title: Fur-back
Name: Fairy Tales
Media: Colour pencil, soft pastel

This is a mixture of the beauty of Fur fashion and the mystery of Chinese culture. Signature for fur is fox fur which is one of the most elegant skins in the world; the background is a bamboo forest with lights in the morning giving the illustration blur layers. The unique point for this illustration is all done by hand drawing especially the balance of fur and the background and the contrast of hard and soft.

Water Colour

Water colour painting technique is relatively easy among the various painting methods; with various performance methods, it is somewhat similar with gouache, though with weaker ability of coverage than that of gouache.

Its characteristics of transparency and randomness could make it used in the watercolour clothing illustrations. You can use bright colour to cover the bottom in dark colour; you can also increase the richness of tone to meet the needs of delicate clothing illustration. So far, many illustrators have combined the watercolour painting technique with some other techniques and thus have reached perfect results.

⊕ Adddress

Germany

Title: Focused
Media: For each project a different technique is used to
emphasise the theme as well as possible.

The Spring Summer 2010 collection is called "Focused". This is
simply a focus on the details which represent the collection.

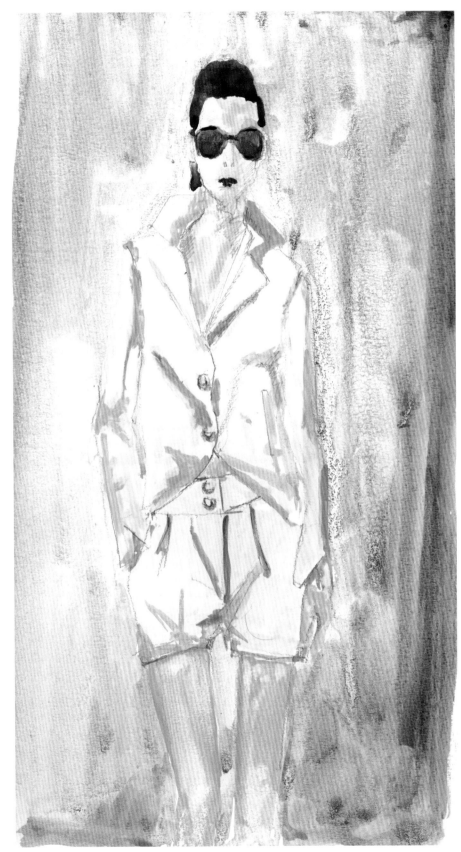

⊕ **Adddress**
Germany

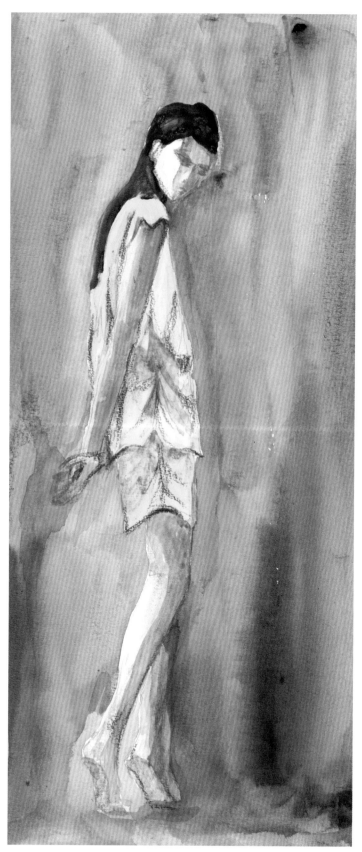

Adddress
Germany

Title: Focused
Media: For each project a different technique is used to
emphasise the theme as well as possible.

The Spring Summer 2010 collection is called "Focused". This is
simply a focus on the details which represent the collection.

⊕ **Adddress**

Germany

⊕ Emmy Mees
Belgium

Title: A Spoon Full of Atmosphere
Media: colour pencil and marker on paper

Illustrations of the atmosphere for the silhouettes of the "A
Spoon Full of Wind " collection inspired on Mary Poppins

⊕ Emmy Mees

Belgium

Title: A Spoon Full of Wind
Media: colour pencil and marker on paper

Illustrations of silhouettes for the "A Spoon Full of Wind"
collection inspired on Mary Poppins.

⊕ **Emmy Mees**
Belgium

⊕ Emmy Mees

Belgium

Title: A Spoon Full of Wind
Media: colour pencil and marker on paper

Illustrations of silhouettes for the "A Spoon Full of Wind"
collection inspired on Mary Poppins

⊕ Emmy Mees
Belgium

Title: A Spoon Full of Wind
Media: colour pencil and marker on paper

Illustrations of silhouettes for the "A Spoon Full of Wind"
collection inspired on Mary Poppins.

⊕ **Emmy Mees**
Belgium

⊕ Emmy Mees
Belgium

Title: Cream White Fashion
Media: colour pencil and marker on paper

Illustration for the magazine Nina
about fashion trends.

⊕ Emmy Mees
Belgium

Title: Orange Cloud
Media: colour pencil and marker on paper

Illustration for the magazine Nina
about fashion trends,

⊕ Emmy Mees
Belgium

Title: Smoking' Strong
Media: colour pencil and marker on paper

Illustration for the magazine Nina about fashion trends.

Title: Highland High Design
Media: colour pencil and marker on paper

Illustration for the magazine Nina about fashion trends.

⊕ **Emmy Mees**
Belgium

Title: Fashionable Light Shopping
Media: colour pencil and marker on paper

Illustration for the magazine Nina
about fashion trends

⊕ Emmy Mees
Belgium

Title: New Years Eve Dances through Some Fancy Snacks & Drinks
Media: colour pencil and marker on paper

Illustration for the magazine Nina
about health

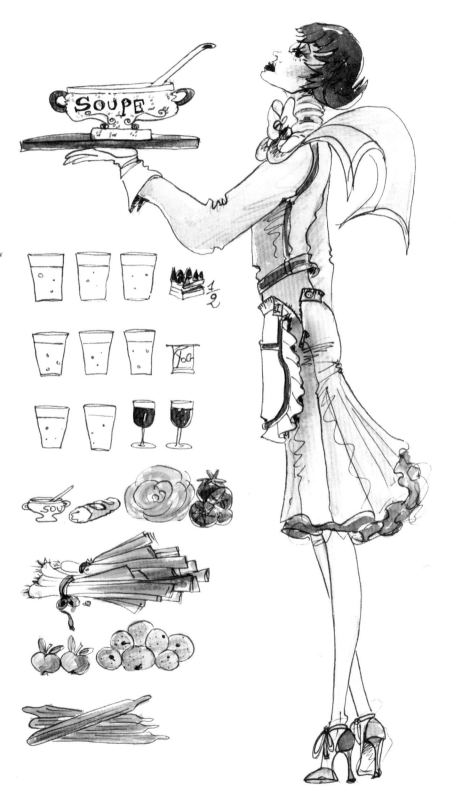

⊕ Emmy Mees
Belgium

Title: A la Française
Media: colour pencil and marker on paper

Illustration for Feeling Magazine about how
the French keep their weight.

⊕ **Emmy Mees**
Belgium

Title: Handle with Care
Media: colour pencil and marker on paper

Illustrations of the silhouetttes of the "Watch out I'm too hot to handle" collection based on fire and golfing ladies.

⊕ Emmy Mees

Belgium

Title: Hole in One
Media: colour pencil and marker on paper

Illustrations of the silhouettes of the "Watch out I'm too hot to handle" collection based on fire and golfing ladies.

⊕ **Emmy Mees**
Belgium

Title: Lightning Dame
Media: colour pencil and marker on paper

Illustrations of the silhouetttes of the "Watch out I'm too hot to handle" collection based on fire and golfing ladies.

⊕ Emmy Mees
Belgium

Title: Vulcano
Media: colour pencil and marker on paper

Illustrations of the silhouetttes of the "Watch out I'm too hot to
handle" collection based on fire and golfing ladies.

⊕ Emmy Mees
Belgium

Title: Burning Desire for Power
Media: colour pencil and marker on paper

Illustrations of the silhouetttes of the "Watch out I'm too hot to
handle" collection based on fire and golfing ladies.

⊕ **Emmy Mees**
Belgium

Title: Too Hot to Handle Styled Heads
Media: colour pencil and marker on paper

Illustrations of the make-up and styling of the "Watch out I'm
too hot to handle" collection based on fire and golfing ladies.

⊕ **Emmy Mees**

Belgium

Title: Too Hot to Handle Styled Heads
Media: colour pencil and marker on paper

Illustrations of the make-up and styling of the "Watch out I'm
too hot to handle" collection based on fire and golfing ladies.

⊕ Emmy Mees
Belgium

123

⊕ **Emmy Mees**
Belgium

Title: Too Hot to Handle Styled Heads
Media: colour pencil and marker on paper

Illustrations of the make-up and styling of the "Watch out I'm too
hot to handle" collection based on fire and golfing ladies.

⊕ **Emmy Mees**
Belgium

⊕ **Emmy Mees**
Belgium

Title: Too Hot to Handle Styled Heads
Media: colour pencil and marker on paper

Illustrations of the make-up and styling of the "Watch out I'm
too hot to handle" collection based on fire and golfing ladies.

Emmy Mees
Belgium

⊕ **Ewelina Klimczak**
  Poland

FASHION

⊕ **Ewelina Klimczak**
Poland

⊕ **Agnes Dorosz**
Canada

Title: Simone
Media: watercolour, coloured pencil, ink

This drawing is all about trying to capture the folds in beautiful pink fabric through the use of watercolour mixed with coloured pencil accents.

⊕ **Agnes Dorosz**
Canada

Title: Gabrielle
Media: watercolour, coloured pencil, ink

"Through the use of smooth textures with sharp and dark lines I
wanted to show the sharp contrast of the fabric against her skin
and hair. "

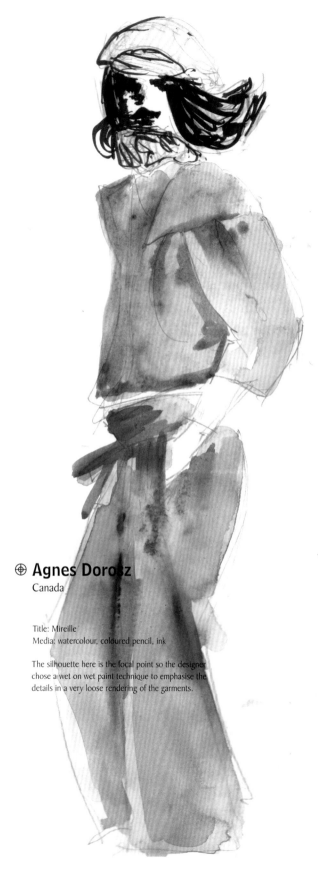

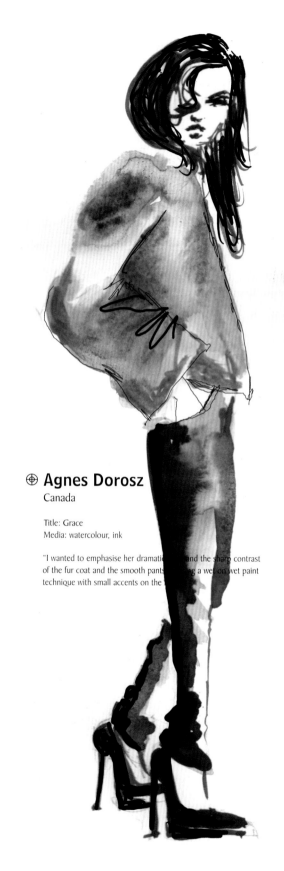

⊕ **Agnes Dorosz**
Canada

Title: Mireille
Media: watercolour, coloured pencil, ink

The silhouette here is the focal point so the designer chose a wet on wet paint technique to emphasise the details in a very loose rendering of the garments.

⊕ **Agnes Dorosz**
Canada

Title: Grace
Media: watercolour, ink

"I wanted to emphasise her dramatic and the sharp contrast of the fur coat and the smooth pants a wet on wet paint technique with small accents on the

⊕ Agnes Dorosz
Canada

Title: Luisa
Media: watercolour, Photoshop

"I love how classic and elegant her jacket and skirt are reflecting an almost Edwardian era feeling. After completing the illustration I wanted to tweak the rendering giving the drawing an edgier look by using Photoshop filters."

⊕ **Agnes D orosz**
Canada

Title: Alexandra
Media: watercolour, Photoshop

This dress is so theatrical but the designer also wanted to play with simplifying the facial gestures and lines. After completing the painting she tweaked the details using a Photoshop filter to give the illustration a blended look.

Agnes Dorosz
Canada

Title: Medusa
Media: watercolour, coloured pencil

⊕ Monsieur Qui

⊕ **Monsieur Qui**

⊕ **Merissa Eisener**
USA

Title: The Park
Media: marker on layout paper

Spring collection for a young contemporary customer

Merissa Eisener

⊕ **Merissa Eisener**
USA

Title: Southwest is Best
Media: marker on layout paper

Designs for a young contemporary customer mixing Navajo
and prairie influences.

⊕ **YAN FONG**

Marker Pen

Marker pen is a common painting tool that could quickly express the design concept and draw renderings. It is very popular among the illustrators, owing to its effective expression, various colours and strong attraction.

Usually, the lines drawn with the marker pen are regular which encourage the formation of a unified visual style. Many illustrators would like to use the row pen, point pen, jump pen, vignette blur, blank and other methods to increase the sense of liveliness. Sometimes, marker pen is used with other tools, such as the coloured pencil, water colour and so on to create magical effects.

⊕ **Elena Kikina**
Germany

Title: Firkant
Medium: pencil, Adobe Photoshop

✦ **Elena Kikina**
Germany

⊕ **Elena Kikina**
Germany

Title: Schnittstelle
Medium: felt pen/pencil, Adobe Photoshop

⊕ **Elena Kikina**
Germany

Computer software

Computer software gives the illustrator a hand to express his creativity.
Both traditional media effects, such as oil paintings, watercolours, prints
and digital graphics' endless styles, new interest can be achieved easily
and rapidly.

⊕ **Anne Marie Maniego**
USA

PERFECT

couture

⊕ **Anne Marie Maniego**
USA

Title: Perfect 10 Couture
Media: hand drawn using Prismacolour coloured pencils,
Prismacolour markers, Prismacolour pastels, edited it Photoshop
using filters and textures

PERFECT 10 BEAUTY TEE: Illustrator – live trace, all vectors,
and gradients; INSPIRATION: Beauty of a Perfect 10 woman;
FOR: Perfect 10 Couture's graphic tee collection.

by: anne marie maniego

by: Anne Marie Maniego

⊕ **Anne Marie Maniego**
USA

Title: Perfect 10 Couture
Media: Hand drawn using Prismacolour coloured pencils,
Prismacolour markers, Prismacolour pastels, edited it Photoshop
using filters and textures

PERFECT 10: Illustrator – all vectors; INSPIRATION: Perfect 10
Couture's logo and ideal Perfect 10 woman; FOR: Perfect 10
Couture's fashion graphic tee collection.

⊕ Anne Marie Maniego
USA

Title: Hellz Girl
Media: hand drawn using Prismacolour coloured pencils,
Prismacolour markers, Prismacolour pastels, edited it Photoshop
using filters and textures.

ILLUSTRATION: Illustrator – all vectors; INSPIRATION: Hellz
Bellz model in the designer's own interpretation of a confident
woman with her own unique "swag".

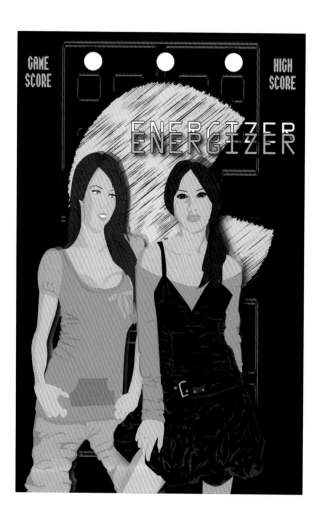

⊕ Anne Marie Maniego

USA

Title: Energizer Illus
Media: Hand drawn using Prismacolour coloured pencils,
Prismacolour markers, Prismacolour pastels, edited it Photoshop
using filters and textures

ILLUSTRATION: Illustrator – all vectors; INSPIRATION: 80's
classic arcade games (PAC MAN); FOR: FIDM Portfolio, Spring/
Summer '09 Juniors Sportswear collection.

anne marie young maniego
209.923.0359 | amymaniego@yahoo.com

⊕ Anne Marie Maniego

USA

Title: Energizer Illus 2
Media: Hand drawn using Prismacolour coloured pencils,
Prismacolour markers, Prismacolour pastels, edited it Photoshop
using filters and textures

ILLUSTRATION: Illustrator – all vectors; INSPIRATION: 80's
classic arcade games (PAC MAN); FOR: FIDM Portfolio, Spring/
Summer '09 Juniors Sportswear collection.

⊕ Anne Marie Maniego
USA

Title: Design Is
Media: hand drawn using Prismacolour coloured pencils,
Prismacolour markers, Prismacolour pastels, edited it Photoshop
using filters and textures

ILLUSTRATION: Illustrator – all vectors; INSPIRATION: 80's classic
arcade games (PAC MAN); FOR: FIDM Portfolio, Spring/Summer '09
Juniors Sportswear collection.

⊕ Anne Marie Maniego

USA

Title: Miranda Kerr
Media: hand drawn using Prismacolour coloured pencils,
Prismacolour markers, Prismacolour pastels, edited it Photoshop
using filters and textures

ILLUSTRATION: Illustrator – all vectors; INSPIRATION: Miranda
Kerr on the cover of BAZAAR fashion magazine; FOR: personal
work.

⊕ **Brenda Dos Santos Szeto**
USA

Title: Fashion Illustration
Media: Adobe Photoshop and Adobe Illustrator

This design is inspired by a Heering vintage cocktail drink.

⊕ **Brenda Dos Santos Szeto**
USA

Title: Fashion Illustration
Media: Adobe Photoshop and Adobe Illustrator

This design is inspired by a Heering vintage cocktail drink.

⊕ Divya Raman
UK

⊕ Divya Raman
UK

Title: Telecommandments
Media: graphite pencil, Photoshop- Lasso tool, Corel Draw, graphic pen, felt tips

Fashion Illustrations Spring/Summer 2011

⊕ **Divya Raman**
UK

⊕ **Divya Raman**
UK

Title: Telecommandments
Media: graphite pencil, Photoshop- Lasso tool, Corel Draw,
graphic pen, felt tips

⊕ **Divya Raman**
UK

⊕ **Divya Raman**
UK

Title: Telecommandments
Media: graphite pencil, Photoshop- Lasso tool, Corel Draw,
graphic pen, felt tips

TRANSLATE
HUMANOIDS

we imitate machines
and we make machines
imitate us

⊕ **Fabiana Pigna**
Los Angeles, CA

Title: Caballo Viejo
Media: Adobe Illustrator

Inspired by Carmen Miranda's head dress, this seudo-abstract version reads "Caballo Viejo" or "Old horse" a popular Venezuelan folk song.

⊕ **Fabiana Pigna**
Los Angeles, CA

Title: Agyness
Media: Adobe Illustrator and Photoshop

A digital portrait of model Agyness Dein wearing
a felt and chain neck piece.

⊕ Fabiana Pigna
Los Angeles, CA

Title: Spring Delirum
Media: pencil and Adobe Photoshop

A mixed media creation of the designer's Spring 2009 collection of flirty dresses tops and skirts.

⊕ **Fabiana Pigna**
Los Angeles, CA

Title: Majas
Media: pencil and Adobe Photoshop

A mixed media creation of the designer's Fall 2009 collection
inspired by Southern Spain heritage and pizzaz.

⊕ Muhammad Fawad Noori
Pakistan

Title: CAD-Illustration
Media: Adobe Illustrator and Adobe Photoshop

"While working on the collection for brand terracotta,
I decided to make a presentation on computer.
First I started making outline of illustration by using
Adobe Illustration then did rendering and finished
the illustration by using Adobe Photoshop. It is very
informative and creative to make illustration by using
these softwares."

⊕ **Leonard Cadient**

Michael

⊕ **Leonard Cadient**

jason WU

⊕ **Leonard Cadient**

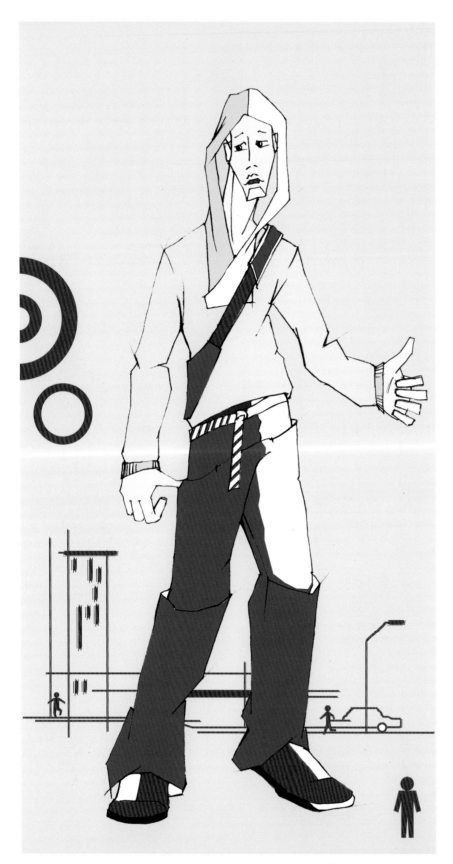

⊕ **Nadja Hermann**

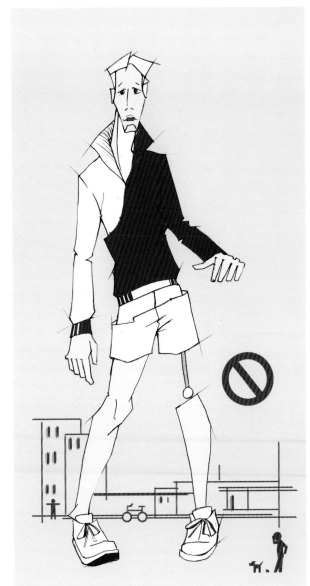

⊕ Nadja Hermann

For the Images "Look left… Look right…" the inspiration had been found in the city of central London, on the streets, in the traffic, the constant hurry, the colourful environment and incredible force of concentrated creative energy. Another inspiration for that was the designer's interest in works by David Hockney and his colour pallet.

Sandra Vandermerwe

Title: Personal Fashion Folio Illustration
Media: pencil, ink pen, Photoshop

178

⊕ **Sandra Vandermerwe**

179

⊕ **Sandra Vandermerwe**

Title: Personal Fashion Folio Illustration
Media: pencil, ink pen, Photoshop

⊕ Sandra Vandermerwe

Title: Fashion Illustration for Abercrombie & Fitch
Media: pencil, ink pen, acrylic, Photoshop

Title: Fashion Illustration for Filleo
Media: ink pen, photoshop

⊕ Sandra Vandermerwe

Title: Fashion Illustration for Abercrombie & Fitch
Media: pencil, ink pen, Photoshop

⊕ **Sandra Vandermerwe**

Title: Spring 2010 fashion illustrations for Juicy Couture
Media: pencil, ink pen, Photoshop

⊕ **Sandra Vandermerwe**

⊕ Sandra Vandermerwe

Title: Key Looks Fashion Illustration for Abercrombie & Fitch
Media: pencil, ink pen, Photoshop

⊕ **Sandra Vandermerwe**

Title: Key Looks Fashion Illustration for Abercrombie & Fitch
Media: pencil, ink pen, Photoshop

⊕ **Sandra Vandermerwe**

⊕ Sandra Vandermerwe

⊕ Sandra Vandermerwe

Title: Key Looks Fashion Illustration for Abercrombie & Fitch
Media: pencil, ink pen, Photoshop

Tele-commandments

⊕ **Divya Raman**
UK

Title: Telecommandments for a Cathodic Soul
Media: Adobe Photoshop, Illustrator, Graphic Montage

Telecommandments explores graphic narratives by the fusion of lenticular animation and digital textile print. Her design ideology employs digital technology in fashion as a toy and tool.

⊕ Divya Raman
UK

Title: Telecommandments for a Cathodic Soul
Media: Adobe Photoshop, Illustrator, Graphic Montage

Telecommandments explores graphic narratives by the
fusion of lenticular animation and digital textile print. Her
design ideology employs digital technology in fashion as
a toy and tool.

⊕ **Divya Raman**
UK

Title: Telecommandments for a Cathodic Soul
Media: Adobe Photoshop, Illustrator, Graphic Montage

Telecommandments explores graphic narratives by the fusion of lenticular animation and digital textile print. Her design ideology employs digital technology in fashion as a toy and tool.

Tele-commandments

Tele-commandments

⊕ **Divya Raman**
UK

Title: Telecommandments for a Cathodic Soul
Media: Adobe Photoshop, Illustrator, Graphic Montage

Telecommandments explores graphic narratives by the
fusion of lenticular animation and digital textile print. Her
design ideology employs digital technology in fashion as
a toy and tool.

⊕ **Divya Raman**
UK

Title: Paper Planes
Media: Adobe Illustrator, Graphic Montage

Spring/Summer 2010 Collection explores childhood innocence with
edgy silhouettes at play.

paper planes
ss 2010

⊕ **Divya Raman**
UK

Title: D Bunk
Media: Adobe Photoshop, graphite Pencil, Graphic
Montage

Spring summer 2002 Active-wear inspired collection

DIVYA RAMAN
COLLECTION : D BUNK SS02

Collage

Collage is a more casual and diversified technique which varies in the colour, texture as well as the materials. Collage works are generally used as decorations. It is in line with the needs of the clothing illustrator that to have a distinct personality characteristics, strengthen the theme of the design, to express the emotion of the clothing illustrator and present the distinctiveness and novelty of the fashion clothing.

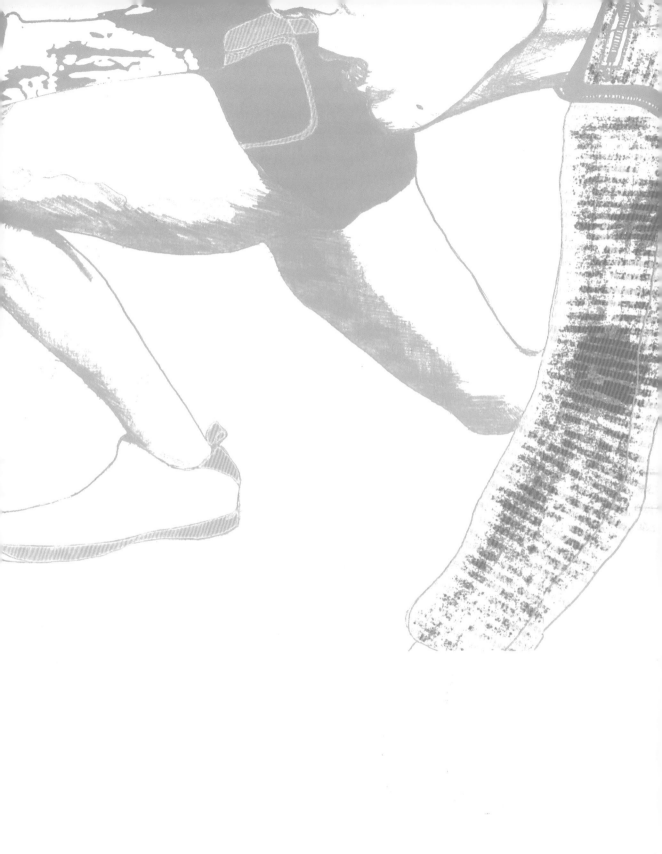

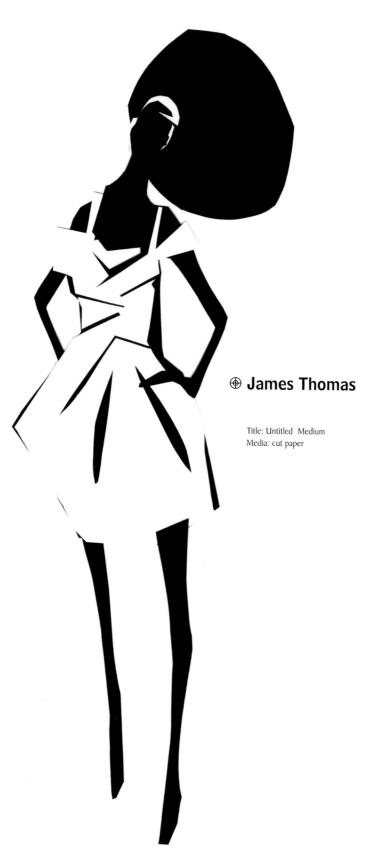

⊕ **James Thomas**

Title: Untitled Medium
Media: cut paper

⊕ James Thomas

Title: Untitled Medium
Media: cut paper

⊕ **James Thomas**

Title: Untitled Medium
Media: cut paper

⊕ **James Thomas**

Title: Untitled Medium
Media: cut paper

⊕ **James Thomas**

Title: Untitled Medium
Media: cut paper

⊕ **James Thomas**

Title: Untitled Medium
Media: cut paper

⊕ **James Thomas**

Title: Untitled Medium
Media: cut paper

⊕ **James Thomas**

Title: Untitled Medium
Media: cut paper

⊕ Paul Nelson-Esch
Portugal

Title: Hot Rod Girl
Media: pencil, ink, pantone and mixed media

Inspired by the "Hot Rod and Surf Guitar" music, films and the fashion scene that came out of Southern California in the early 1960's. The sounds of Dick Dale and his Deltones, girls in bikini's, surfboards and hot roding action.

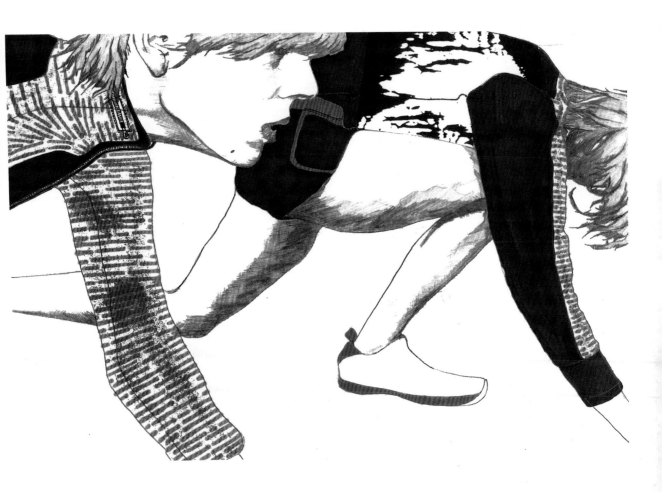

⊕ Paul Nelson-Esch

Portugal

Title: Puma
Media: pencil, ink, pantone and mixed media

A collection that was inspired by and designed for
Puma in 2000, but was never used.
The idea was to cross high performance sportswear with
street fashion, to create a forward-looking sportswear
collection.

⊕ **Paul Nelson-Esch**
Portugal

Title: Puma
Media: pencil, ink, pantone and mixed media

A collection that was inspired by and designed for
Puma in 2000, but was never used.
The idea was to cross high performance sportswear with
street fashion, to create a forward-looking sportswear
collection.

⊕ Paul Nelson-Esch

Portugal

Title: Channel Earth
Media: pencil, ink, pantone and mixed media

Inspired by a distorted view of fashion from an alien
perspective. The idea is that we are being watched
from another planet through television. A slanted angle,
asymmetrical design and cuts on the bias.

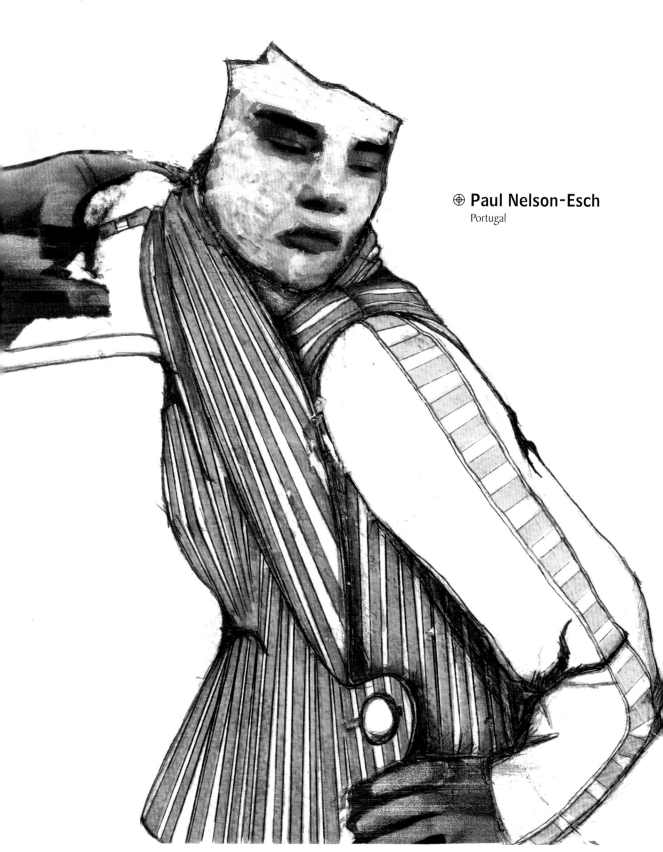

⊕ **Paul Nelson-Esch**
Portugal

⊕ Paul Nelson-Esch

Portugal

Title: Stylevice
Media: pencil, ink, pantone and mixed media

A mix of the smooth 1980's sounds and "Cappucino Kid" fashion of "The Style Council" and the pastel pink, blue and pistachio pin striped suits of "Miami Vice's" Crockett and Tubbs.
The pin stripes are reinvented and the pastels are electrified.

⊕ **Paul Nelson-Esch**
Portugal

⊕ Paul Nelson-Esch
Portugal

Title: Stylevice
Media: pencil, ink, pantone and mixed media

A mix of the smooth 1980's sounds and "Cappucino Kid" fashion of "The Style Council" and the pastel pink, blue and pistachio pin striped suits of "Miami Vice's" Crockett and Tubbs.
The pin stripes are reinvented and the pastels are electrified.

215

⊕ **Paul Nelson-Esch**
Portugal

⊕ Paul Nelson-Esch
Portugal

Title: Indian Wars
Media: pencil, ink and mixed media

Native American costume during the wars of the late
1800's crossed with British regimental uniforms from
the Crimean war. The idea of strict regimental uniforms
being reinterpreted and used in a tribal way and then
reinvented for a modern catwalk.

⊕ **Paul Nelson-Esch**
Portugal

Title: L.A. to Vegas
Media: pencil, ink, pantone, glitter pens and mixed media

An American roadtrip through time. Starting in Los
Angeles in the 1980's with the inspiration of Motley Crue
and Poison and the glam metal music scene. Finishing at
the International Hotel in Las Vegas in the 1970's with
Elvis Presley. It is all lip gloss, mascara, gold sequins and
jumpsuits.

⊕ **Paul Nelson-Esch**

Portugal

Title: Summer Afternoon Nap
Media: handmade paper, fabric, pen, Photoshop

Knitted striped top and denim shorts.

Synthetical techniques

As a derivative of modern painting art, clothing illustration is different from other purely creative arts, but it also has a certain value of art appreciation. The creation of clothing illustration could be seen as the continued exploration of the art of painting. Till now, there are many creative styles of the clothing illustration. The synthesised technique is quite free which gives the illustrator a hand to express his/her creativity.

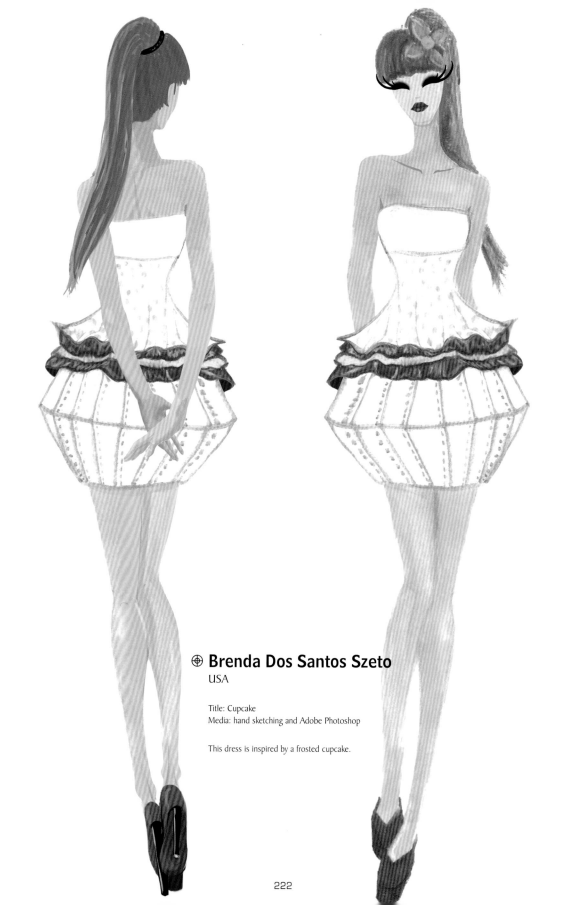

⊕ Brenda Dos Santos Szeto
USA

Title: Cupcake
Media: hand sketching and Adobe Photoshop

This dress is inspired by a frosted cupcake.

⊕ Carsten Juhl
Denmark

Title: Wedding Dress
Media: ink pen, marker and crayon on paper

Design and illustration by Carsten Juhl

⊕ **Carsten Juhl**
Denmark

Title: Wedding Dress
Media: ink pen, marker and crayon on paper

Design and illustration by Carsten Juhl.

CARSTEN JUHL 05.05

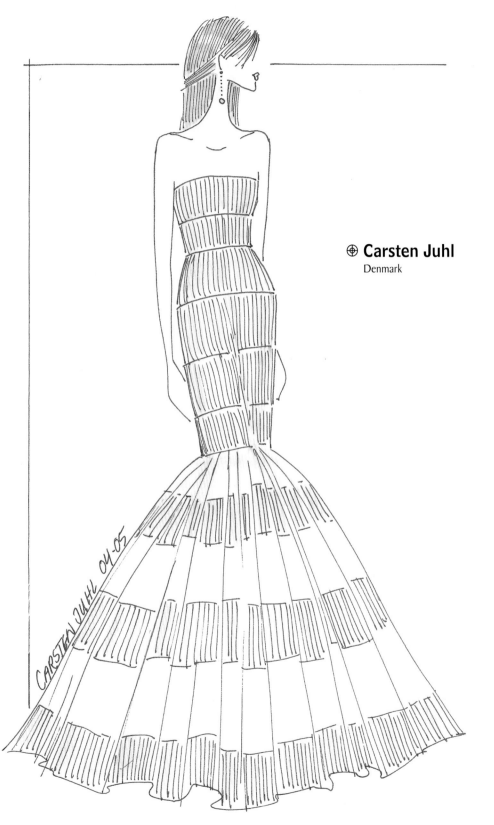

⊕ **Carsten Juhl**
Denmark

CARSTEN JUHL 04-05

⊕ **Carsten Juhl**
Denmark

CARSTEN JUHL 05.05

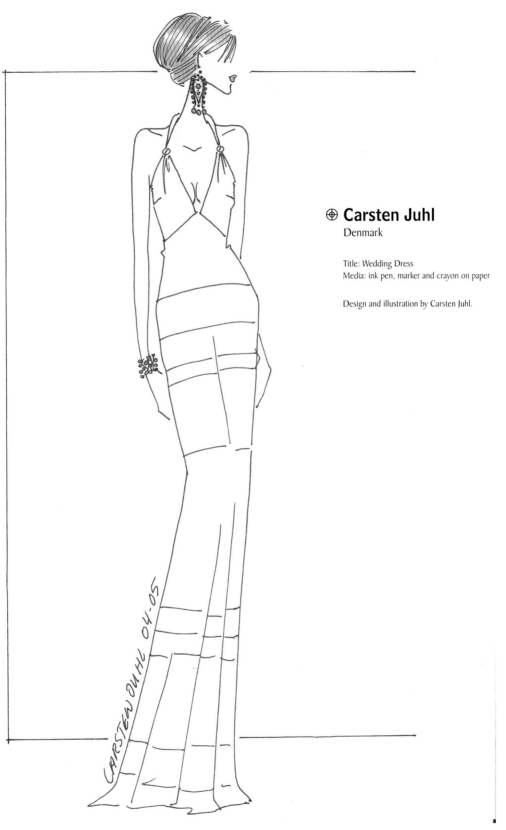

⊕ **Carsten Juhl**
Denmark

Title: Wedding Dress
Media: ink pen, marker and crayon on paper

Design and illustration by Carsten Juhl.

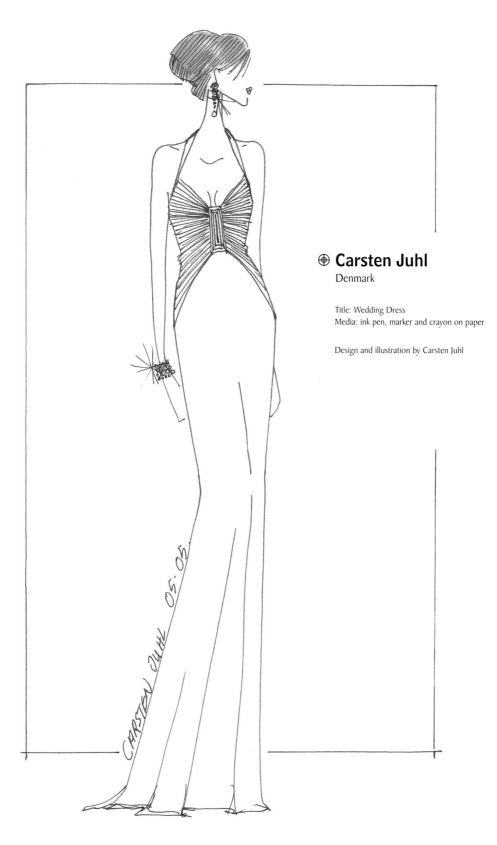

⊕ Carsten Juhl
Denmark

Title: Wedding Dress
Media: ink pen, marker and crayon on paper

Design and illustration by Carsten Juhl

⊕ **Carsten Juhl**
Denmark

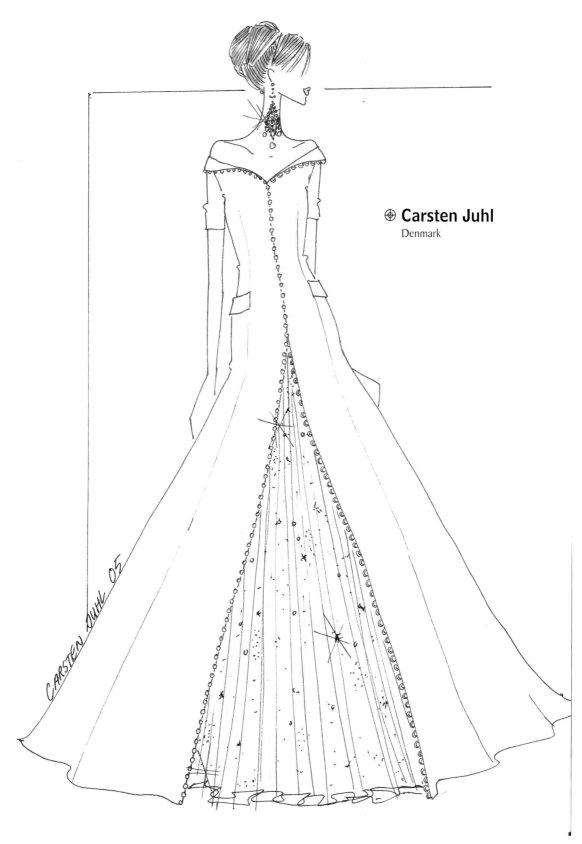

⊕ **Carsten Juhl**
Denmark

CARSTEN JUHL 05

⊕ Carsten Juhl
Denmark

Title: Wedding Dress
Media: ink pen, marker and crayon on paper

Design and illustration by Carsten Juhl.

⊕ **Carsten Juhl**

Denmark

⊕ Carsten Juhl
Denmark

Title: Wedding Dress
Media: ink pen, marker and crayon on paper

Design and illustration by Carsten Juhl

⊕ **Carsten Juhl**
Denmark

Title: Evening Dress
Media: ink pen, marker and crayon on paper

Design and illustration by Carsten Juhl

Carsten Juhl

Denmark

Title: Cape and Evening Dress
Media: ink pen, marker and crayon on paper

Design and illustration by Carsten Juhl for Copenhagen Artificial Fur.

⊕ Carsten Juhl
Denmark

Title: Stole and Cocktail Dress
Media: ink pen, marker and crayon on paper

Design and illustration by Carsten Juhl for Copenhagen Artificial Fur.

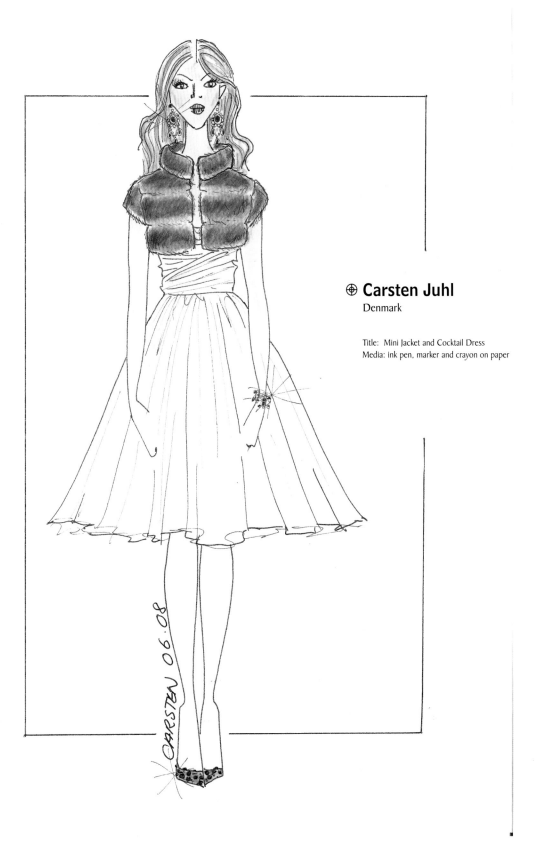

⊕ **Carsten Juhl**

Denmark

Title: Mini Jacket and Cocktail Dress
Media: ink pen, marker and crayon on paper

⊕ **Carsten Juhl**
Denmark

Title: Jacket and Evening Dress
Media: ink pen, marker and crayon on paper

Design and illustration by Carsten Juhl for Copenhagen Artificial Fur.

⊕ **Carsten Juhl**
Denmark

Title: Jacket and Wedding Dress
Media: ink pen, marker and crayon on paper

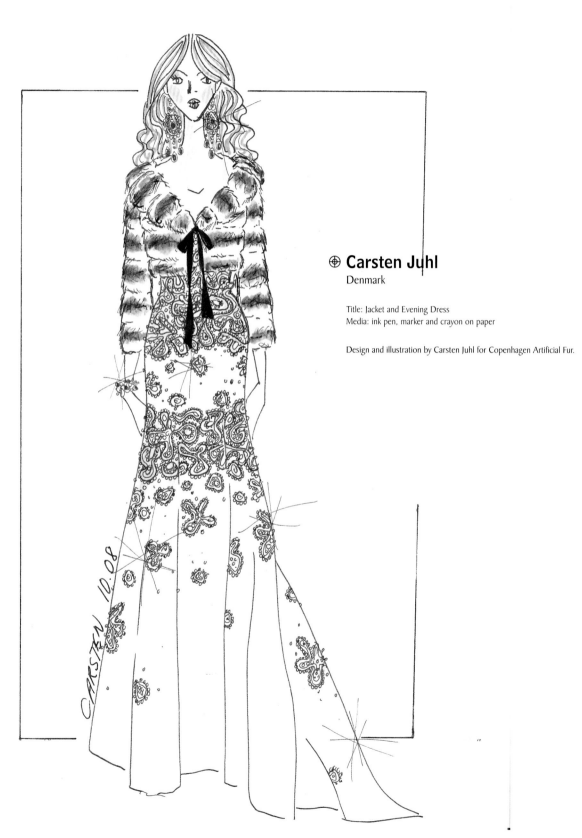

⊕ **Carsten Juhl**
Denmark

Title: Jacket and Evening Dress
Media: ink pen, marker and crayon on paper

Design and illustration by Carsten Juhl for Copenhagen Artificial Fur.

⊕ **Carsten Juhl**

Denmark

Title: Jacket and Evening Dress
Media: ink pen, marker and crayon on paper

CARSTEN 07.08

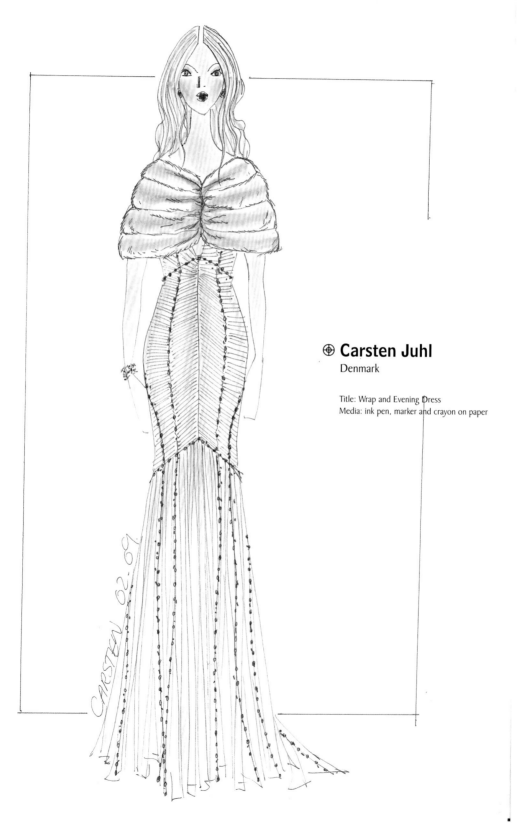

⊕ **Carsten Juhl**

Denmark

Title: Wrap and Evening Dress
Media: ink pen, marker and crayon on paper

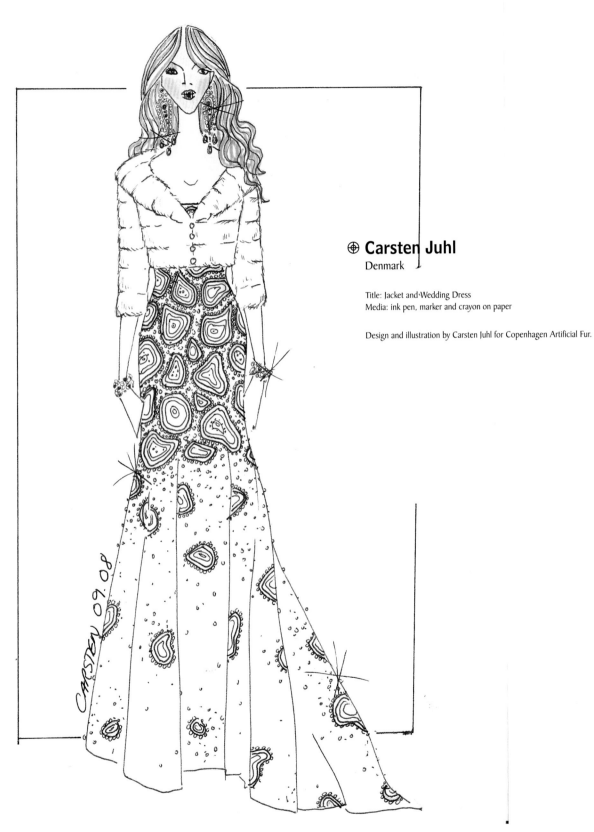

⊕ **Carsten Juhl**
Denmark

Title: Jacket and Wedding Dress
Media: ink pen, marker and crayon on paper

Design and illustration by Carsten Juhl for Copenhagen Artificial Fur.

CARSTEN 09.08

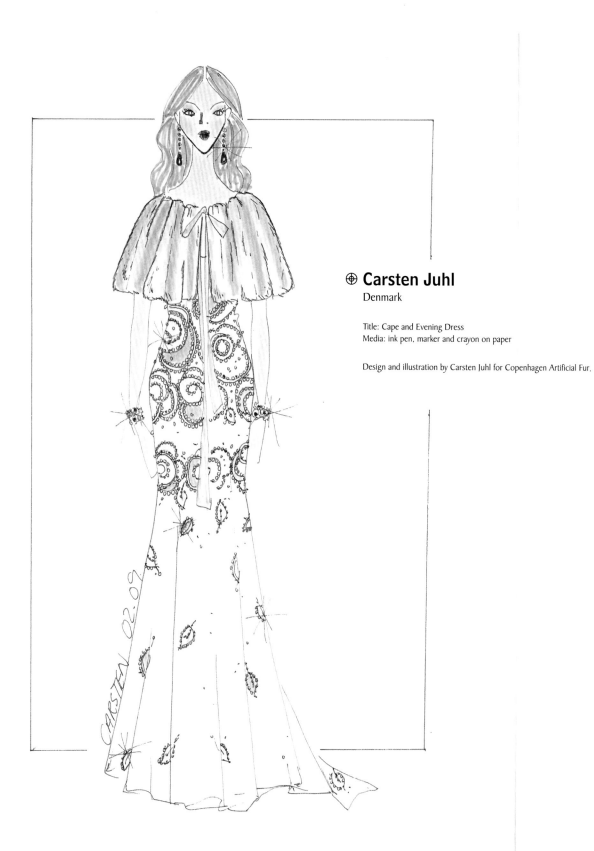

⊕ **Carsten Juhl**
Denmark

Title: Cape and Evening Dress
Media: ink pen, marker and crayon on paper

Design and illustration by Carsten Juhl for Copenhagen Artificial Fur.

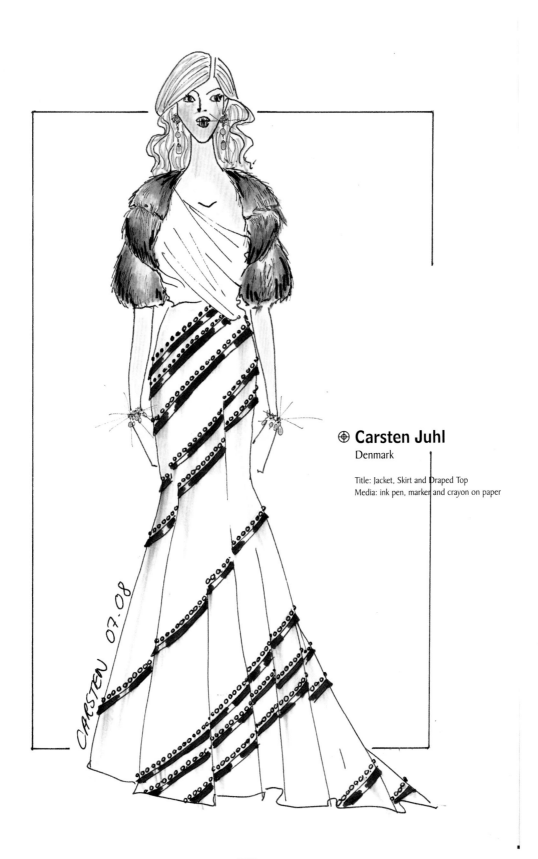

⊕ **Carsten Juhl**

Denmark

Title: Jacket, Skirt and Draped Top
Media: ink pen, marker and crayon on paper

CARSTEN 07.08

⊕ Carsten Juhl
Denmark

Title: Draped Tops and "Ink" Pattern Bottoms
Media: study in draping, paper on paper, ink on white
paper napkin, ink pen

Design and illustration by Carsten Juhl, study in draping.

⊕ **Carsten Juhl**
Denmark

Title: "Ink" Pattern Dresses
Media: paper on paper, ink pen and ink on white paper
napkin, inverted colours

Design and illustration by Carsten Juhl

⊕ **Carsten Juhl**
Denmark

Title: Evening Dress with Fur Detail
Media: paper on paper and decoupage, inverted colours

Design and illustration by Carsten Juhl.

⊕ Carsten Juhl
Denmark

Title: Draped Top and Skirt
Media: paper on paper and ink pen, inverted colours

Design and illustration by Carsten Juhl.

⊕ Carsten Juhl
Denmark

Title: Goth Fantasy
Media: ink pen on paper

Design and illustration by Carsten Juhl.

⊕ **Carsten Juhl**
Denmark

Title: Goth Fantasy
Media: ink and crayon on paper

Design and illustration by Carsten Juhl, study in
medieval armour.

⊕ **Muhammad Fawad Noori**
Pakistan

Title: African Brides Collection 1 (Formal)
Media: mix media (water colour markers, poster colours,
        pointers, water colours, etc.)

"That was my mockup exam of final year, and the theme
which I have selected is African Bride. I have designed two
collections: one is formal and the other is casual. Three outfits
have been designed under formal section including Bridal
dress. It was a great learning experience to do work under
pressure. The medium used in this is mix media (water colour
markers, poster colours, pointers, water colours, etc.)."

ROBE DE GRAND'SOIR

Muhammad Fawad Noori

Pakistan

Title: African Brides Collection 2 (Casual)
Media: mix media (water colour markers, poster
        colours, pointers, water colours, etc.)

"This is the casual wear collection under the same
theme. I have designed two outfits: one is day wear
jacket with skirt and the other is vest with pants. The
whole project was amazing, very learning especially
when doing rendering and body paint. It was a very
good experience while working different categories
of the same theme. The medium used in this is
mix media (water colour markers, poster colours,
pointers, water colours, etc.)."

⊕ **Muhammad Fawad Noori**
Pakistan

Title: Futuristic
Media: poster colours and marker & pointers

"When I was working on this illustration while rendering it my brush was slipped and a bad stroke was made on back of this illustration. Then suddenly I added more strokes of that kind to balance the whole composition. I have designed party wear dress for winter season using leather patches. It was another kind of experience."

⊕ Muhammad Fawad Noori
Pakistan

Title: On Ramp
Media: pointers and markers & water colours

"Once a day, I was watching fashion show on TV. Suddenly I decided to make an illustration with the title "on ramp" and so I made this master piece. The media I have used to drawn this illustration is Pointers, Markers and watercolours. It was a great experience to combine them in such a way. Only the colour red has been used in very less amount since it is a black and white & line work."

⊕ **Tunstullstudio**

⊕ **Tunstullstudio**

⊕ **Katherine Tuttle**

New York, USA

Title: AstroGlam
Media: rendered in marker, coloured pencil, enhanced with Photoshop

⊕ **Katherine Tuttle**
New York, USA

Title: AstroGlam
Media: rendered in marker, coloured pencil, enhanced with Photoshop

Katherine Tuttle
New York, USA

Title: Shoes
Media: rendered in marker and coloured pencil, background Photoshop

⊕ **Katherine Tuttle**
New York, USA

⊕ **Katherine Tuttle**
New York, USA

⊕ **Katherine Tuttle**
New York, USA

⊕ **Katherine Tuttle**
New York, USA

Title: Napoleon
Media: rendered in marker, coloured pencil, graphite

⊕ **Katherine Tuttle**
New York, USA

Title: Napoleon
Media: rendered in marker, coloured pencil, graphite

⊕ **Katherine Tuttle**
New York, USA

⊕ **Katherine Tuttle**
New York, USA

Katherine Tuttle
New York, USA

⊕ **Katherine Tuttle**
New York, USA

Title: Napoleon
Media: rendered in marker, coloured pencil, graphite

⊕ **Katherine Tuttle**
New York, USA

⊕ Katherine Tuttle
New York, USA

⊕ **Katherine Tuttle**
New York, USA

Title: Crane
Media: rendered in graphite, tissue paper background

⊕ **Katherine Tuttle**
New York, USA

Title: Crane
Media: rendered in graphite, tissue paper background

⊕ Lucy Brickwood
UK

Title: Madness in Blue
Media: Indian ink, oil pastel and pencil line drawing on layout paper

This project is from the collection "could it be madness – this?" 2008.
Lucy Brickwood,UK. The illustration is pencil line drawing on paper.

⊕ **Lucy Brickwood**
UK

Title: Burlingtons Heritage Army
Media: acrylic ink with latex on card

This image is for "heritage" collection 2007 for Burlington, UK.
They are acrylic ink with latex blotted on paper. This collection was about British heritage, focusing on empowering women inspired by castles as well as armour which are reflected in both the silhouette as well as the textiles used.

⊕ Lucy Brickwood
UK

Title: Bags of Bedlam
Media: Indian ink, oil pastel and pencil line drawing on layout paper

This project is from the collection "could it be madness – this?" 2008
by Lucy Brickwood,UK. The illustration is pencil line drawing on paper.

⊕ Lucy Brickwood
UK

Title: Beauty of linsanity
Media: Indian ink, oil pastel and pencil line drawing on layout paper

⊕ Lucy Brickwood
UK

Title: Flight of Fancy
Media: pencil and colour pencil drawing and pastel on paper, Photoshop collage

This illustration was for the "flight of fancy" collection 2009 for Ell and Cee, UK-based brand. (www.ellandcee.co.uk)
Pencil and colour pencil drawing and pastel on paper, Photoshop collage.
Flight of fancy is a 1920s inspired graceful, romantic, vintage feel collection couture lingerie with beautiful delicate details.

⊕ Lucy Brickwood
UK

Title: Screaming Bouclier
Media: Indian ink, oil pastel and pencil line drawing on layout paper

This project is from the collection "could it be madness – this?" 2008
by Lucy Brickwood, UK. The illustration is pencil line drawing on paper.

⊕ Lucy Brickwood

UK

Title: The Modern Roger Chaplin
Media: promarker on paper

Illustration from "eccentric cavalier" collection
of Mattimo Dutti, 2008, Spain.
This illustration is promarker on paper.
The collection is based on the classic well-
dressed chic menswear, the swarve style of
Roger Moore's 007 sleek British style and
Savile row tailoring and fabrications with a
Charlie Chaplin fit and silhouette.

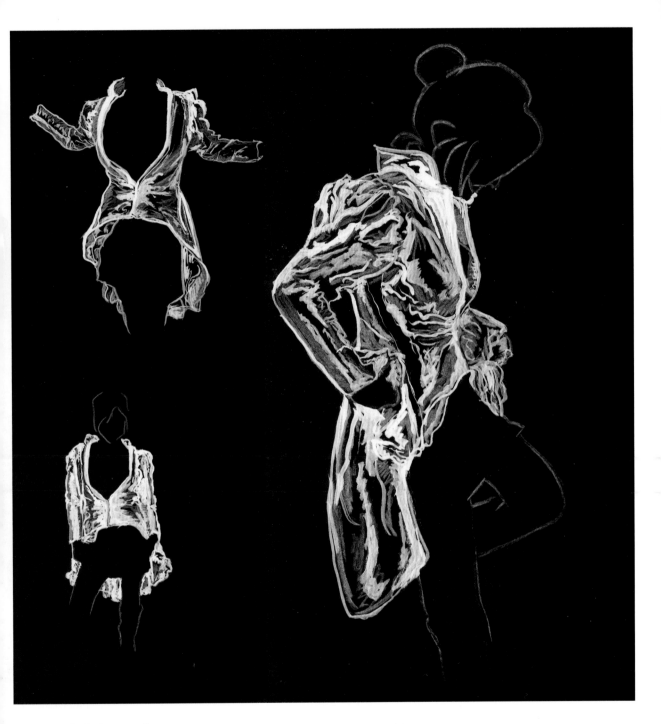

⊕ **Lucy Brickwood**
UK

Title: Snow White
Media: white pencil, ink chalk and paint on black card

Illustrations for Tiffin for "sexed up panto" collection 2007 UK.
This was created with shades of white pencil, ink, paint and pastel on black
card. The collection was a small tailoring collection based on comedy
figures from pantomime, giving them a new more modern edge.

⊕ **Merissa Eisener**
USA

Title: Adventure Bound
Media: Illustrations were done individually with marker and coloured pencil on linen paper and combined into one layout in Adobe Photoshop.

Collection of women's sportswear inspired by collectible Hummel Figurines.

⊕ Nadja Hermann

The two "new" images have been inspired by one of the designer's favourite books, "Hard-boiled Wonderland and the End of the World" by Haruki Murakami. The designer loved the idea of the two parallel worlds, one of which is the real world, the world of high technology and business in modern Tokyo, the other one being the world of imagination, the world of nature, origin and fantasies.

⊕ **Nadja Hermann**

⊕ Nadja Hermann

The series "sport women" are inspired by the designer's experiences of living in Toronto and Berlin, by the similarities of the two cities and their differences, by the street fashion there, music and urban life style.

⊕ **Nadja Hermann**

Lavender
snakeskin
or
ostrich
skin

Antique
gold
metal
clasp

*Oversized
herringbone print
*RAW EDGE
REVERSE PATTERN
CROSSFRONT DRESS

⊕ **Robyn Smith**

USA

Title: Fall 2011
Media: marker, coloured pencil and gouache

The design concept behind these designs, stemmed from taking shapes
and colours often associated with designs from1980's and reworking them
in a more up-to-date silhouette by using geometric shapes and all
over printed graphics.

⊕ Robyn Smith
USA

Title: Valentina
Media: pencil, marker, coloured pencil and some Photoshop retouching

"Random design ideas. In addition to creating a sexy woman who embodies the aesthetic of the kind of woman I would want to wear my clothes. I want to have different types of models, Black, White, Asian, etc. for my future clothing," Robyn Smith said.

Ingredients:
- Raw edges
- deep V's
- Buttons (various sizes)
- Flowy Tops that could double as mini dresses
- skinny jeans w/ leggings
- large topstitching
- Piping

Self fabric Piping or Leather piping @ pocket openings 1/4"

self fabric piping around straps.

gathered hem

pocket curved flap

cuffed trouser shorts

⊕ **Robyn Smith**
USA

Title: Summer Time Chic
Media: pencil and marker and some Photoshop retouching

The idea behind this set of illustrations was that the designer was creating some light/airy summer time looks for Summer 2009. The concept is chic, fun and flirtatious.

artwork/ graphic
printed on top of
knit
raw edge

65% Cttn
35% Satin
knit

mixed
media
knit +
woven

⊕ Robyn Smith

USA

Title: The Girls
Media: pencil, marker and coloured pencil and some Photoshop
retouching

This was just a collage of random design ideas and illustrations that
the designer imagined. The bird is her favourite part of the sketch...
The designer likes to add different elements in the drawings, which
force the viewer to study each part of her illustration carefully.

⊕ Robyn Smith
USA

Title: Red
Media: pencil, marker, gouache and some
Photoshop retouching

Using colour to evoke the feeling of excitement.
The paint splatters represents sudden, quick,
uncontrollable movements. The woman in the
illustration is only halfway filled with colour
because she is not the focus. The focus is the
shoes and the geometrically shaped bag the
designer designed. Done in a striking shade of
bright red, the awkward posing of the model
enhances the intensity of design and overall
layout.

⊕ **Robyn Smith**
USA

Title: I Love Shoes
Media: pencil drawing with markers and coloured pencil, and some Photoshop retouching

"Simply... My love for shoes. I wanted to portray a woman in a provocative pose, where she appears to be in a day dream like state thinking about her love for shoes. She loves her shoes so much she couldn't even decide which pair to wear so she put on two different shoes," Robyn Smith said.

⊕ **Robyn Smith**

USA

Title: Mirror Mirror
Media: markers and coloured pencil

"I am constantly looking in a mirror, checking myself out, so I decided to illustrate a woman looking in the mirror touching up her eye make up. A simple black and white line drawing with pops of colour. I am also interested in getting a tattoo so all of my girls have tattoos. I am basically sketching out my tattoo ideas in my illustrations," Robyn Smith said.

Robyn Smith
USA

Title: Boing
Media: pencil drawing with markers/quache paint and coloured pencil,
and some photoshop retouching

The idea behind this illustration was to use different human body parts and
place them in awkward positions, mixed with the designer's futuristic shoe
designs. Shoes that take you to outer space... metal bouncing coils as shoe
soles/heels. The shoes and the purse are the fashion elements. The entire
image takes your eyes on a rollercoaster ride. It forces you to look at every
aspect of the drawing. Some of the designer's illustrations often hide hidden
messages (drawings within drawings, words in the hair, etc.), so you have to
really study the illustration.

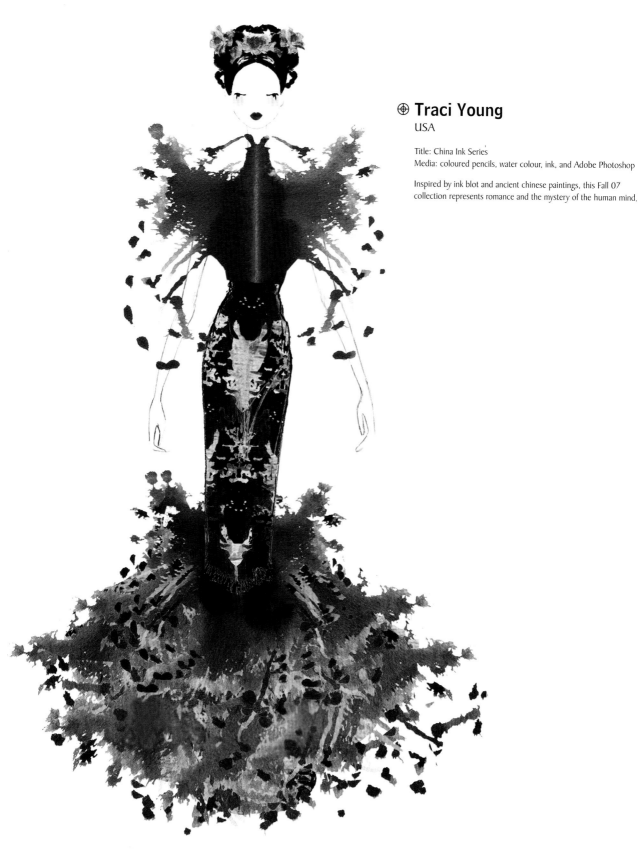

⊕ **Traci Young**
USA

Title: China Ink Series
Media: coloured pencils, water colour, ink, and Adobe Photoshop

Inspired by ink blot and ancient chinese paintings, this Fall 07 collection represents romance and the mystery of the human mind.

⊕ **Traci Young**
USA

⊕ **Traci Young**
USA

⊕ Traci Young
USA

Title: China Ink Series
Media: coloured pencils, water colour, ink, and Adobe Photoshop

Inspired by ink blot and ancient chinese paintings, this Fall 07
collection represents romance and the mystery of the human mind.

INDEX

Adddress
Email: contact@adddress.de
Website: www.adddress.de

Agnes Dorosz
Email: agnesdorosz@gmail.com

Alexandra Kaegler
Email: info@alexandrakaegler.com
Website: www.alexandrakaegler.com

Anca Georgiana Lungu
Email: psiloula@yahoo.com

Anne Marie Maniego
Email: Anne_Moniego@gap.com
      annemarieym@gmail.com

Brenda Dos Santos Szeto
Email: brenda@brendadss.com
Website: www.brendadss.com

Carsten Juhl
Email: Carstenjuhl@gmail.com
Website: www.carstenjuhl.com

Divya Raman
Email: designisdigital@gmail.com
Website: www.coroflot.com/divyaraman

Elena Kikina
Email: kikina@firkant.de
Website: www.elena-kikina.de
      www.wearfirkant.com

Elmaz Hüseyin
Email: elmaz_huseyin@mindspring.com
Website: www.elmazhuseyin.com

Emmy Mees
Email: emmy.mees@telenet.be
Website: www.emmymees.com

Ewelina klimczak
Email: ewe-k@hotmail.com
Website: www.ewelinaklimczak.carbonmade.com

Fabiana Pigna
Email: fabiana.pigna@gmail.com

James thomas
Email: jamesathomas@mac.com
Website: www.paulnelsonesch.carbonmade.com

Lucy Brickwood
Email: ljbrickwood@gmail.com

Merissa Eisener
Email:meisener@gmail.com
Website: www.coroflot.com/meisener

Nadja Hermann
Email: hermannn@gmx.de
      info@nadja-hermann.com
Website: www.nadja-hermann.com/

Neda Niquie
Email: Design@NIQUIE.com
Website: www.niquie.com

Paul Nelson-Esch
Email: paulnelsonesch@gmail.com
Website: www.notjustalabel.com/paulnelsonesch

Robyn Smith
Email: missnotoriousrobyn@gmail.com

Sandra Vandermerwe
Email: sandy_van2000@yahoo.com

Shīvani Gakhar
Email: shivanigakhar@gmail.com
Website: www.coroflot.com/shivanigakhar

Tiffany Fitzgerald
Email: TSFitzgerald@comcast.net
      Tiffany@TiffanyFitzgerald.net
Website: www.tiffanyfitzgerald.net

Traci Young
Email: couturekitty@gmail.com
Website: www.coroflot.com/traci_young

Yan Fong
Email: yuyanfong@gmail.com
Website: www.yanfong.net